Women as Elders:
The Feminist Politics of Aging

Women as Elders:
The Feminist Politics of Aging

Edited by
Marilyn J. Bell

Women as Elders: The Feminist Politics of Aging was simultaneously issued by The Haworth Press, Inc., under the title: *Women as Elders: Images, Visions, and Issues* and simultaneously published as a special issue of the journal *Women & Politics,* Volume 6 Number 2, Summer 1986, Marilyn J. Bell, guest Editor.

Harrington Park Press
New York • London

ISBN 0-918393-34-5

Published by
Harrington Park Press, Inc., 12 West 32 Street, New York, New York 10001

EUROSPAN/Harrington, 3 Henrietta Street, London WC2E 8LU England

Harrington Park Press, Inc., is a subsidiary of the Haworth Press, Inc., 12 West 32 Street, New York, New York 10001.

Women as Elders: The Feminist Politics of Aging was originally published as *Women & Politics*, Volume 6, Number 2, Summer 1986.

Cover design by Marshall Andrews.

Library of Congress Cataloging-in-Publication Data

Women as elders.

"Originally published in 1986 by the Haworth Press, Inc. It has also been published as Women & politics, volume 6, number 2, 1986."
Includes bibliographies.
1. Ages women—Congresses. 2. Aged women—Religious life—Congresses. I. Bell, Marilyn J.
HQ1061.W643   1986b   305.4   86-25696
ISBN 0-918393-34-5

CONTENTS

Contributors

Gert Beadle is a 70 year old feminist poet who has published three books of poetry since age 60 when she became involved in feminist issues. During that time she has also been instrumental in establishing Women's Crisis Homes, Incorporated, including a women's centre, rape and sexual assault crisis line, women's health collective, women's credit union, a feminist newspaper and Norther-Women. She helped establish women's centres in Attikakan, Canora, Fort Frances and currently serves on the board of the women's center in Kelowna. She is a 1986 recipient of the Order of Canada and received the Person Award in 1984.

Nancy Breeze is a white, 55 year old, Florida Crone whose natural habitat is the St. Augustine sand dunes. She has contributed age-affirming articles to *Prime Time*, *Broomstick* magazine, *Hot Flash*, and the special issue on aging of *Southern Exposure*. A graduate of Michigan State University, she has been active in the Displaced Homemaker movement, conducted menopause workshops, and is a member of the Older Women's League.

Karla F.C. Holloway is an Associate Professor of English at North Carolina State University and holds a PhD from Michigan State University. She is Associate Editor of *Obsidian II* a journal of Black literature and critical theory. Her book, *The Character of the Word: The Texts of Zora Neale Hurston* is forthcoming in 1987 to be followed by *New Dimensions of Spirituality: A Bi-Racial Reading of the Novels of Toni Morrison* which she has co-authored with Stephanie Demetrakopoulos.

Stephanie Demetrakopoulos is a feminist theologian and philosopher, Professor of English at Western Michigan University with her PhD from the University of Minnesota. She has published widely on images of women in literature and the depth psychology of spiritual development in women. She is author of *Listening to Our Bodies: The Rebirth of Feminine Wisdom*, has co-authored, with Karla

Holloway, *New Dimensions of Spirituality: A Bi-Racial Reading of the Novels of Toni Morrison* which is forthcoming and is currently working on a book which will address the spiritual aspects of women's addictions and recoveries.

Rita L. Margraff, MA, GNSH, has been a member of the Grey Nuns of the Sacred Heart for 25 years and currently serves as Administrator of the Grey Nuns Motherhouse in Yardley, Pennsylvania. The Motherhouse complex is the headquarters for the Grey Nuns but also houses the retirement facilities for this Congregation of religious women. She holds a Master's degree in mathematics from Villanova University and has completed various courses in gerontology in conjunction with her present employment.

Jean M. Coyle is President of Jean Coyle Associates, a gerontological consulting firm in Alexandria, Virginia. She is Founding President of the International Association of Gerontological Entrepreneurs, a Vice President of the National Alliance of Homebased Businesswomen, member of the Board of Directors of the Network of Entrepreneurial Women, and former Chair of the Women's Studies Council at Eastern Illinois University. Dr. Coyle has served on the faculty of Northeast Louisiana, Eastern Illinois, George Mason, Howard and Texas Women's Universities and the University of Southern Indiana. She holds a PhD in Sociology.

Doris B. Hammond has a PhD in Counseling from the University of Georgia and is an Associate Professor of Psychology and Director of the Gerontology Graduate Program at D'Youville College, Buffalo, NY. She has made numerous presentations to professional groups as well as being an invited speaker at conferences relating to sexual and health concerns of mid-life and older women. She has written on these and related topics and has counseled mid-life and older women.

Terri A. Eisler received her PhD in Family Studies from Virginia Polytechnic Institute and State University where she held the position of Director of the Center of Gerontology. She has been coordinator of Women's Services at Northeastern Illinois University in Chicago. Currently, Dr. Eisler is Assistant Professor of Sociology/Gerontology at D'Youville College, Buffalo, NY. Her research interests include: career development in women, second careers, assertiveness training for women, commuter marriages and families with developmentally disabled members.

Della Ferguson is an Associate Professor and Coordinator of the Psychology Department and Assistant Director of the Institute of Gerontology at Utica College of Syracuse University. She is active with GROW (Group for Research on Midlife and Older Women). Her own research interest is major transitions in the lives of midlife and older women, and the accompanying stresses and coping mechanisms.

Kathleen M. Schwede has made presentations and written on women and aging, Supreme Court decision making and women, and women's mental health. She organized a Rape Crisis program in Kalamazoo, Michigan, has been a Women's Program Director in the YWCA, and worked with a collectively run women's bookstore. After a mid-life career change, she is pursuing a Master of Science in Nursing with emphasis on mental health.

Marilyn J. Bell is an Associate Professor of Sociology and Chairperson of Social Sciences at D'Youville College in Buffalo, NY. Over the last ten years she has focused her research, writing and presentations on elder women with particular interest in the feminism and empowerment of elder women, elder women as depicted in children's magazines and detective fiction, and elder women in women's spirituality. She received her PhD in Sociology from Western Michigan University.

PREFACE

The Nature of Crones

It is in the nature of a Crone to lean to overview, for she is in a reflective period of her life and the big picture has her attention. She has walked in many moccasins not her own and has observed that all pinch and restrict the natural desire for freedom. This recognition of the sameness in the female condition allows her to cross freely over lines that the paternal system has encouraged in order to label and divide. A Crone's vision of the future demands the vitality of contrast in both color and texture that boldly speaks of the individual being true to her own spirit. She believes that spirit is on the side of justice and compassion and lends itself to the struggle for change, both internally and externally in the world in which she lives. Among the things she has labelled excess baggage are organized religion and its many patriarchal prophets. Unwilling even now, though, to consign the male to excess baggage, she chooses a kinder term, ''distraction of my youth'' that no longer moves me to sympathy. As a matter of fact she has little sympathy to give either sex, choosing empathy to her own sex as a value term. She observes the sweat of materialistic society and the ideology of militarism which has superceded all other ideologies as an extension of patriarchal thought and in her innermost imaginings would create a separate nation on the best of feminist philosophy and a return to nature.

The Crone does not participate in the politics of reform; her bag is transforming the thought processes that interfere with the civil rights of spontaneous persons with creative gifts. She is distinguished by her ability to dream dreams and conjure up visions for the survival of the Web, weaving into the fabric a lively wit that refuses to take seriously the small mind, loaded with self-righteous hyperbole, or conversely, the professional academic drowning in self-

xiii

analysis. Her instinct for survival is at gut level, she has solved the problems of want by wanting little, possessions have little value to the true Crone. She lives to live, to speculate and to risk, she will not be found in the nest of privileged security or at the table of greed or envy, she has pared her life down to the minimum. She will speak for peace but not expect it, speak for love, but not bet on it, speak for harmony among women knowing how far off is the reality, but she will speak, for she is a spinner of possibilities, a teller of truths too long avoided. She will sit in the councils of women in defense of other women and nurture the common need, for this is her chosen family, over even her natural family, for the councils speak the language of women which few men understand. A Crone is nurtured by the energy her words create, inspired by their ability to make music and laughter out of disappointment and grief, so powerful are these words in their imagery, so vulnerable in their indecision. In this time and this place they are invincible.

Yet it is in the company of other Crones a serenity occurs. There is such quiet strength in the faces of those who cannot be seduced by privilege or bought by expediency to deny what they know. There is such comfort in the presence of those who have never conformed to the patriarchal image of women as appendages but stubbornly pursued a course of independent action, while being open to every experience of life, including such amusement as the trials and tribulations that tested our wits and stiffened our spines.

There is a coven like quality in this gathering of Hags who have embarrassed and harassed the powerful into responding to their demands, who have refused to be silenced by a thrown bone, or discouraged by the lack of female support or impressed by belated congratulations. We have a history of resistance to drink to, Courageous Crones with only one adversary yet to face, the male spectre death, and we shall have to meet him alone on his terms. We have discussed it, we fear only a delayed resolution. Our work is done but our voice is not stilled, our investment long term but secure. The Crone makes few judgments, she has been sensitized to both the pain and pleasure of life, she has protected herself from neither, nor would she wish to deprive anyone else of the wisdom inherent in both. As women, our strength is in each other. We must nurture that strength to create the music that all would choose to dance to.

Gert Beadle
Web of Crones
Kelowna, British Columbia

Introduction

This symposium is for every woman who reads it, and for every male reader who has any significant women in his life. The issues are our issues, the images are us—now or as we may present ourselves in the future—the visions and the dreams must be ours as we bring the future into the present. We are aging, we will be old. We will confront the issues of health, economic security and social support systems in all their configurations. We will live with our images, the stereotypes of old women, the mythology of our lives, and our secret knowledge of ourselves as the persons we really are. We dream the future. We envision the life we expect and the life we desire.

Our culture gives us many images from grandmothers in Norman Rockwell magazine covers to bag ladies on street corners to adolescent mentalities in aged bodies on TV sitcoms. Our policy makers, until very recently, assumed we would be provided for by our husbands. Our religious institutions gave us theology which sees women as valuable only for procreation, not the activity of the aged. Our medical and mental health professionals describe a limbo between menopause and death. This is not the "stuff" of our dreams, it is the "stuff" of our issues.

In the academic realm, few writers of text books address elder women at all. A quick review of text materials in women's studies, be they generic works or those specific to a discipline, will immediately show the reader that little is included regarding elder women; a few paragraphs on the empty nest syndrome, menopause, depression in middle age, or the lack of older women in the women's movement seems to suffice. A similar situation can be found in gerontology texts, again specific in areas such as social gerontology, psychology of aging, economics of aging or generic introductory survey texts. A few paragraphs on widowhood appear, perhaps mention of menopause or depression. The research underlying the theories of aging has often not even included women.

Nancy Breeze and the Crones Nest Committee have provided a vision. These women are working to provide community for elder women. They envision a residential alternative inclusive of women from various life styles, racial/ethnic groups, manifesting a range of economic and health conditions. Through research, consciousness raising, networking, these women have moved to planning and designing. The vision is not yet the reality; as are women the vision is growing and maturing. We cannot move in next week, but we can expand our dreams to include such alternative possibilities in the future.

Although the Crones Nest is the only project of this type included in the symposium, other groups of women have been talking of similar alternatives. I have heard these discussions, for some years now, in social and professional settings. Sometimes the focus is on urban elder women and the transformed apartment building: other times it is the rural "back to the land" vision. Women know they will probably outlive their husbands. Most do not envision and dream living with their adult children. Some have neither husbands nor children to weave into future visions. The new vision is that of creating our own alternative residential communities, designed with sensitivity to the needs—physical, emotional and spiritual—of the projected resident community.

Karla Holloway and Stephanie Demetrakopoulos, drawing on the rich tapestry of Toni Morrison's writings, move us into the area of images. They examine the elder Black women in the context of the political and the spiritual: as the givers of life and strategizers of survival. These Black foremothers are seen through the African heritages as well as the American Black experience; they "assume the mythology of Africa and become magical in their wisdom." They are "matriarchy accomplished rather than 'in process'. . . . "

This article is a unique collaboration, as well as an important addition to literary analysis of Black writers and their fictional characters; it is in part co-authored in the usual sense while other sections are by one or the other of the authors. Holloway is young and Black, Demetrakopoulos is middle-aged and white. Both are academics. In their writing, Holloway and Demetrakopoulos blend the traditional academic approaches with what might be termed improvisional imaging. Themes are never lost and throughout there is a blend of African rhythms, Greek goddess archetypes and American experiences. Each, in solo performance, spins a thread of Morrison's characters, her own life and the elder women who have impacted on it. The perceptions are not always the same. Cultural differences in the way Black and white perceive and interpret the feminine and aging as well as the aging female are evident. It is in these contrasts and insights that the richness of the article is found. The elder woman as wise, strong, resourceful, the strategist of survival, unites the diversity as the improvisations build to a united voice in optimistic conclusion. Optimism is called for not only in terms of aging, but also in the sense that we really can, as Holloway and Demetrakopoulos have, overcome the differences of culture, age, race and academic specialities. Neither author has lost her own unique voice in the process, yet seldom is the common bond that unites women so clear.

Sister Rita Margraff, MA, GNSH, introduces another bonding of women, that of the religious congregation and the issues being faced by such groups as their memberships age. It should come as no surprise to lay readers that young women are not entering religious orders in large numbers at this time in our history. Nor are we surprised any longer by statistics which point to the overall aging of our society. Readers not close to religious congregations of women, however, are not likely to have given thought to the rapidly changing age structure within these groups and the problems raised by such a disproportionately aged community. Margraff reviews the cultural values and socialization within religious congregations and demonstrates how these are reflected in the later years. Three congregations are described in terms of their efforts to resolve the age structure problems. Themes of retirement, career changes, housing, medical care and economic security which emerge at the beginning of the article are reconsidered for the future.

Although this work addresses the concerns of a very specific subculture among women, the questions of an aging population confront us all. The cultural values of an already aged population are different within a religious order, yet many of the patterns can be found among lay women in the larger society as well. The difficulties and the successes religious congregations experience in attempting to resolve the issues of an aged population may serve to provide models in other areas.

Not many women own businesses, yet as Jean Coyle points out, among those who do, almost half are over the age of 50. The major issue of retirement for the women business owners is that it has not been an issue. Little is known about how such women prepare for retirement, adjust to having retired, or avoid the process. In considering the woman business owner, Coyle challenges the stereotypes which would have us believe working women do not invest emotional energy, or derive identity through work, or that retirement is an insignificant issue for working women. She reviews many of the studies of working women and empirical data on retirement to develop questions which need to be raised and some speculative conclusions.

It is a common belief in the social sciences that we seldom have THE answer, the mystical piece of truth which is the definitive statement, but are doing well when we can ask the right question. Certainly this is applicable to the issues of retirement of women business owners. Jean Coyle does not pretend to give us the answers, but seeks to direct our thinking to the right questions.

Doris Hammond focuses our thinking on the issue of health care with critiques of both the level of concern about elder women's health needs, as demonstrated in allocation of research efforts and dollars, and the policy changes being proposed at the federal level. She does not see these proposals as meeting the needs of elder women. While recognizing the work of organizations such as the American Association of Retired Persons, state offices of aging and even the Gray Panthers to develop health policy for all aged, Hammond sees the need for the women's health movement to begin to address the needs of elder women.

She envisions grass roots efforts, similar to those that women developed over such issues as birth control or natural and family centered childbirth, which would focus on the concerns of elder women's health. This political activism would be directed as reform of the current Medicare and to the development of alternatives in health care.

The articles selected for this symposium are diverse and yet they belong together. Just as Holloway and Demetrakopoulos may be improvisations on a common theme within their article, all of the articles are solo improvisations on a common theme: we are the aging women. Most of us do not have lives which parallel Morrison's fictional women; most of us are not Sisters in religious orders; most of us do not own businesses. But, all of us ask the same questions about our future. Margraff, Coyle and Hammond remind us that the answers still have not been developed. We do not know how to insure the security of our later years, our retirement, our health needs. Breeze, Margraff and Hammond each present us with the need to look toward new forms, to develop alternatives, to assert ourselves and take the risks to realize our visions. We may have to do these things. Who else will resolve the issues of the age structure of the convent? Who else will provide health care which public policy does not recognize as our legitimate need? How else will we find a supportive community in which to live rather than a cubicle in "retirement" housing? Holloway and Demetrakopoulos do not provide us with role models from Morrison's work, nor are these elder Black women merely images, but as Holloway and Demetrakopoulos themselves state, the images are "feminist icons, as contributions to the growing canon of 'Lives of the Saints' for women" drawn from literature.

All of these authors challenge us, in one way or another, to analyze the myths, stereotypes and, perhaps especially, the empirical data of patriarchal research carefully. There is an implicit warning to read the labels and instructions completely before swallowing, to be wary of contraindications.

There is a new image of the elder woman being developed. She is strong, wise, dignified as well as playful. She has been a mere shadow in the gerontological literature of previous years. Sometimes she is fleetingly seen as the widow with new found freedom. Other times we catch a glimpse of her as she startles patriarchal researchers by demonstrating life satisfaction while tied to a very small, limited and fixed income. We almost hear her laugh when patriarchal gerontologists, of either sex, portray her negatively as self-centered or eccentric because she has finally reached a point in her life when no one else's needs must come first. Occasionally she stands tall in the public view wearing the face of Georgia O'Keefe, Margaret Mead or Eleanor Roosevelt, Katherine Hepburn or Maggie Kuhn. More often she stands just slightly out of our vision, but frequently present, feeling like our grandmothers or great aunts. Gert Beadle, herself 70, has captured her essence in the "Nature of Crones."

This new elder woman tiptoes in our dreams and our visions. She lurks behind our mirrors, catching our glance briefly and waiting to look us full in the face. If we ask her who will solve our problems and give us the kind of later years we want, she would no doubt chuckle and paraphrase the concluding sentence of Doris Hammond's article: the fact is, and history substantiates, that only through women, ourselves, will the best solutions be found.

Marilyn J. Bell, PhD
D'Youville College
Buffalo, New York

Crones Nest:
The Vision

Nancy Breeze With the Crones Nest Committee

"Mable Turner was really lucky," Grandma said, looking up from her jigsaw puzzle. I imagine I looked surprised as I asked, "Why is that?" "The way she died," Grandma replied firmly. "Last week, when she was whipping up the egg whites for an angelfood cake, she suddenly collapsed. Heart attack. Right there in the kitchen!"

Recently, as I spoke with the members of the Crones Nest Committee, I was reminded of that conversation, back in the forties when electric mixers were less common. Now these St. Augustine, Florida women are working with elder women to create another kind of "luck" for those latter years; the "luck" of living fulfilling, independent, self-defined, lives in community with other women.

This Crones Nest project is indeed visionary today, when older women have few choices concerning where they may live, often being forced out of their own homes into unsafe, isolated, living conditions. According to the Older Women's League (OWL). "The greatest number of bank foreclosures on homes are among older women living alone." Women's Research and Education Institute has found that nearly half of all elderly women, compared with fewer than one in five old men, live on less than $5000 a year. Generally women have no other income than Social Security, but their benefits reflect years of working in the home or at low-paying jobs. Thus women account for 71% of the elderly poor.

The committee chose the name, Crone, because in ancient times that was the revered third stage of a woman's life (nymph to maiden to crone). The Crones Nest is viewed as an expansion of an already-existing women's residential community, the Pagoda, to an intergenerational and interracial space where elder women are honored and respected for their experience and wisdom. The concept of women caring for each other as we age is itself an old one. During the Roman Empire, a system of old age homes was developed, the

7

first in Constantinople by Helen, Mother of Constantine. These were soon common throughout the Mediterranean, funded by private donations. In the nineteenth century a series of cottages, called "Widow's Row" housed poor, old women in Mobile, Alabama. Crones Nest members want to create a place whose physical structure, administration and programming work together to provide an environment of choices and possibilities for the latter years of lesbian and heterosexual women's lives. They are seeking the advice and suggestions of long-living women to help in all phases of the project, including research and design. In this way they hope to establish a true alternative and not merely provide services.

At a time when increasing agism and sexism work to ignore and devalue older women, it is essential to discover ways that women can remain healthy and independent for as long as possible. Alternative housing and health programs must be developed to assist women. Special health care needs of the elderly must be addressed, as well as what "home" means. Communities of young and old living together can provide an alternative to traditional programs which often lead to deterioration of physical, spiritual, and mental health. Both the Older Women's League (OWL) and the editors of *Broomstick*,[1] a national magazine by, for and about women over forty, endorse the Crones Nest project.

Architecturally this home will be a combination of private living quarters, community rooms and spaces for dining, socializing, community gatherings, activities and therapy, a library, classes, athletics, gardening, sitting outside and enjoying pets. Including an infirmary and hospice will ensure that physical infirmities need not result in segregation and that each woman can exercise control over her own death experience.

Organizationally, residents will have the option of active involvement in the decision-making process for running the home. Residents may be on the staff and staff members who are not residents will be encouraged to maintain close working and personal relationships with the residents.

Activities will be responsive to the needs and desires of the residents, fully respecting each woman's right to be as quiet and contemplative, or as active and involved as she chooses. The Crones Nest committee envisions the home as a healing community that provides opportunities for physical, emotional, mental and spiritual health and growth. Some examples include: classes in exercise, music, dance, arts and crafts; sports and physical therapy; spiritual

gatherings, concerts, performances and workshops; group and individual therapy; and meaningful work within or outside the community. In addition, a special effort will be made to provide natural and
holistic health care as an alternative to drugs, to challenge the dominant cultural attitudes on sickness and death, and to deal openly with
fears, beliefs and expectations about aging and dying.

In the words of Barbara Deming, who was a founding mother of
this project, "such a space will be built with a sensitivity to the
needs of aging women's bodies. Will have softened corners, wide
passages, places to mingle, to be alone. Colors. Music. Occupations
for bodies and minds. . . . "

The Pagoda women's spiritual and cultural community seems an
appropriate sponsor for such an organically-designed undertak-
ing. Over its seven years of existence, it has been through many
changes. Begun as an open resort community, offering women's
space, theatre, crafts, concerts, and workshops, it has evolved into a
more formally structured, cooperatively-run, residential one. Presently the 13 residents, aged 22 through 53, include 2 RNs (a geriat-
ric nurse and a mental health nurse) a social worker with experience
in hospice work, a legal advisor, an architect, a therapist, a business
administrator, a computer analyst, a dancer and foundation coordinator, a graphic artist, an ordained minister, and a women's health
care worker. In addition, the 70 members of the spiritual/cultural
center come to stay for varying lengths of time.

The full-time residents, who had not lived together previously,
have been faced with the challenges of land and property owned and
cared for both individually and by the group, in a 110' by 250' area
containing 10 buildings. It was necessary to build trusting close personal and business relationships to deal with the shared possessions
and responsibilities. Some of the problem-solving and brainstorm-
ing processes that have emerged through these experiences are:
meeting facilitation is rotated, decisions are by consensus, hierar-
chical structures are avoided by contracting for jobs, and all work is
paid at the same hourly rate. The business meetings and the regular
group sessions, devoted to community or interpersonal issues of an
emotional nature, are seen as equally valuable. The group gives support to any community member who asks for it.

It was in the summer of 1982 that some Pagoda women began
meeting to further discuss, brainstorm and plan specific tasks and
time frames for the development of the Crones Nest project. They
wished to expand the community to include a residence for older

women, whether physically strong, of whatever color, creed or economic condition, lesbian or heterosexual, who choose to live their lives in community with other women. The three-phase project was defined:

1. stimulate discussion and greater awareness of immediate and long term long-living women's needs;
2. research, coordinate and document, through a slide/tape show, the needs and visions with particular emphasis on health care, housing, and economic issues;
3. establish a model residential community in St. Augustine for long-living women which could be replicated elsewhere.

During the past three years the women of the Crones Nest committee have met regularly, researching and compiling information on the needs of long-living women, designing, planning and setting priorities. They also developed a mailing list and visited local programs and communities already in existence. Throughout this organic process, original ideas, concepts and designs have been refined, and procedures to handle the daily tasks of the project have been developed. Consciousness-raising around the issues of women and aging continues, through discussion, experiential exercise, music and movies. A film series is planned, to share knowledge and encourage interested women to become involved. The first issue of a newsletter, *The Cronicle*, was published in the winter of 1985.

To continue to seek out the voices of elder women the committee is creating a National Advisory Council of Older Women. A National Board of Consultants is also being formed to utilize the expertise and experience of women active in the field of aging.

Significant work has been done on the slide/tape show which, through interviews with women over the age of 62, will document what is currently available and what is needed, especially in the areas of housing and health care. Actual interviews will be used to ensure authenticity and accuracy; filming the interviewees in their environments will further illustrate the day-to-day problems. Besides providing a forum for women to voice their thoughts and share their lives as they age, the types of facilities in use, including home living situations, will be shown. Through use of a documentary style, complex issues will be introduced, and the slides will be accompanied by appropriate poetry and music. These compiled stories of older women who have experienced difficulties, and their insights, can give shape to alternative models. Eventually the show, which will include a summarizing narrative, could be used in fund raising and ultimately duplicated for distribution to other groups and the general public.

As part of the slide/tape show, a questionnaire has been devised to elicit general information on women and aging and suggestions for an ideal women's residential community. Through meetings with women of different races, classes and lifestyles, presently involved in "senior centers," "community care for the elderly" programs, retirement villages, nursing homes or those living in their own homes, the committee hopes to learn how to assist these women to design what they want for themselves and others. Feminists and lesbians under the age of 62, who have given thought to the subject, will also be interviewed.

Much volunteer committee energy has been spent unsuccessfully in submitting grant proposals to various foundations. The rejection by the MS. Foundation was the most disappointing. In their letter to the Crones Nest committee they stated, "the experience of the Pagoda women in working to establish an alternative community for older women will be specific to the Pagoda constituency and will not be replicable by other groups who want to start similar projects for aging women."

The committee is looking for women interested in: serving on the Advisory Council of Older Women, joining the Board of Consultants, participating as possible workers in the future, or supporting the project in other ways. It also welcomes submissions of slides for possible inclusion in the slide/tape show. For a copy of *The Cronicle*, which explains these needs in more detail, please write the Crones Nest Project, 207 Coastal Hwy., St. Augustine, Florida 32084.

REFERENCES

1. The Older Women's League may be contacted at 1325 G Street, N.W., Lower Level B, Washington, D.C. 20005, and *Broomstick, Options for Women Over Forty*, at 3543 18th Street, San Francisco, CA 94110.

Remembering Our Foremothers: Older Black Women, Politics of Age, Politics of Survival as Embodied in the Novels of Toni Morrison

Karla F.C. Holloway, PhD
Stephanie Demetrakopoulos, PhD

ABSTRACT. In this essay we examine the significance and meaning of novelist Toni Morrison's works in terms of American culture, literary originality, Black feminism and women's spirituality. Our essay also exemplifies and examines some differences between a white female's and a Black female's response to specific patterns in Morrison's novels. We especially examine portraits of old Black women and their spiritual/political significance as foremothers whose survival ensured ours, brought us into being, and gives us strategy. We examine the meaning of these portraits of old Black women to both white and Black women. We use several critical frameworks: biographical, sociological, mythological, archetypal and finally theories from Afro-American studies and from women's studies. We also reflect on how Morrison's women have stirred and awakened our own memories of older women in our lives.

INTRODUCTION

Our two main objectives are first, to examine the significance and meaning of novelist Toni Morrison's works in terms of U.S. culture, literary originality, Black feminism and women's spirituality, and second to exemplify and examine some differences between a white female's and Black female's response to specific patterns in Morrison's novels. We will especially examine protraits of old Black women and their spiritual/political significance as foremothers whose survival ensured ours, brought us into being, and gives us strategy.

Toni Morrison has published four novels. These are stories of girls' growths into young womanhood and women's growths into a magical wisdom of age. Morrison's girls—Pecola, Claudia and Freida (*The Bluest Eye*, 1970)[1]—battle physical and spiritual abandonment, rape/incest and insanity either first hand or by learning that such things happen and discovering the responses of the Black women in the community to such events. Her young women—Sula and Nel (*Sula*, 1973)[2] Jadine (*Tar Baby*, 1981)[3] and Hagar (*Song of Solomon*, 1977)[4] discover that their femaleness entitles them to a certain position in the community but that with this entitlement, individual rights are often abrogated as their membership in this community is refined. Barbara Christian writes that this community in Morrison's novels "presents worlds that are very much like villages in which kinship ties are woven into the dreams, legends, the subconscious of the inhabitants."[5] These communities, like the African clans they represent, exact a certain price for membership. Its women are especially vulnerable to its structure, because their responsibility is to assure the legacy of the clan through the birthing and nurturing of the children. The bonding of the clan in the U.S. reinforced even further the critical role of the mother, because her children represented continuity of life in conditions where life itself was constantly threatened. The mother's role grew to encompass a kind of parenting that was able to survive socioeconomic depression, nutritional deficiencies and political repression. It is critical to Morrison's schema that we understand this African-American woman as sister to African women and "join the scholars who interpret the Black woman in terms of Black (African) social reality."[6]

The older women in Morrison's work and in Black culture bring the African traditions to full fruition. Morrison's older women—Pilate and Circe (*Song of Solomon*), Aunt Jimmy and M'dear (*The Bluest Eye*), and Eva (*Sula*)—fully assume the mythology of Africa and become magical in their wisdom. They don the robes of matriarchy accomplished rather than "in-process," as during the childbearing years, and are thus invested with the knowledge and means to assure that the Black American evolution of the African clan survives its uprooting and reimplantation on foreign and hostile ground. Morrison herself writes that "If anything I do, in the way of writing novels or whatever I write, isn't about the village or the community . . . then it isn't about anything . . . which is to say, the work must be political."[7] These older women are magical because of their will to survive, because of their embodiment of the mythology and wisdom of Africa, and because Morrison invests them with physical qualities larger than life that structure the politics of their survival, and in consequence the survival of the Black community. Morrison writes of the presence of these ancestral figures as a "sort of timeless people whose relationships to the [other] characters are benevolent, instructive, and protective, and they provide a certain kind of wisdom."[8]

Morrison's clan is a complexity of values and mythologies. The presence of the ancestor is critical to its legacy and its promise and therefore blends the traditions of Africa with the contemporary realities of the U.S. Considering the prevalence of agism in white America, one can even see the African traditions as diametrically opposed to U.S. traditions. Black feminism does not have to fight against the denigration of older women within Black culture the way that white feminism must, although in the larger U.S. community, old women of any ethnic background are lumped into negative categories. Age within Black culture, then, is not so much a social issue as it is a mythic and political issue. This is an odd admixture, when seen in terms of traditional sociological perspectives; but, such traditional perspectives are inadequate because of their base in westernized chauvinism. Janice Hale notes that Black child rearing, a critical role of the women within the clan, must resolve conflicts between a European world view and an African world view. She discusses the opposition of a Euro-American ethos where "survival of the fittest" is the operating principle and an African ethos, where both "survival of the tribe" and "oneness with nature" are the operant cultural values.[9] The cultural schism that stems from such worldviews is the primacy of the collective clan vs. the superiority of the individual. A political view of age transmutes in Morrison to a view that encompasses the community, the culture and especially the Black woman as she spiritually and physically carries the survival of the clan. Within her own culture, Morrison does not have to establish the worth of the old woman; that worth is a priori.

Considering the above, the reader can well understand why in this article we have written separately on these issues, examining the reasons behind our different readings of Morrison and highlighting our cultural differences as possible explanations for our perspectives. Karla Holloway's views on Morrison's concepts of the extended family and ideals of womanhood are connected to the issues of racial memory and African archetypes which are possibly her unconscious backgrounds for certain interpretations. Stephanie Demetrakopoulos' views stem from her own ethnic background and studies more typical of white feminists (more on hers later). In addition, we have discovered through our collaboration a way for Black and white women to share their lives and values while acknowledging these to be very different.

This article grew out of literary discussions likely to occur between two women whose friendship began where we met, as two professors in the same English department. We began writing a literary analysis of Toni Morrison; then we saw that differences in interpretations often reflected our ethnic backgrounds—a middle-aged white woman's (Demetrakopoulos, who is a specialist in Renaissance literature and women's studies) and a young Black woman's (Holloway, who is a specialist in linguistics, black literature and modern critical theory). So we began to address our cultural and racial differences directly. Our readings emphasized both African and feminine archetypes; and we found ourselves describing a dimension of female spirituality and psychology hitherto underrepresented in literary studies. Aspects of feminine thealogy (thea is the word for goddess) seemed increasingly a critical feature in our readings. The older Black woman in Morrison's works particularly represents these dimensions as she is the contemporary embodiment of the ancient goddesses, ancestral spirits and earth-mothers. The older Black woman may even be in a sense the ground of being for this aspect of woman's metaphysics. John Mbiti notes that the prayers of African religions are addressed to god as male and female (mother of men) and that a secondary and critical level of prayers features the spirits of departed ancestors, because "the traditional concept of the family, according to African peoples, is one that includes the living, those yet to be born and the departed." To neglect the spirits would "upset the harmony of life."[10]

Our writing was memory and analysis—both of which probed the structure and substance of how Morrison writes, and of how we responded. We wrote in passion, sometimes in gut-wrenching conflict, in love and anger, for the love of the subject and its deepest meaning to us. We wrote unaware of the anger it would provoke toward us and its potential. We were, upon reflection, shielded during our writing by the female intimacy and understandings that can occur when two women work together. As we remembered women in our historical pasts whose lives and living had touched and ensured our own, women in our mythical past became as focused. These archetypes, their values and status, defined not only the structure of our analysis, but rooted it firmly in a feminist history. We claim this project as a cultural legacy that took us far into the philosophical history of our respective civilizations. For the rest of this essay our voices will be separate, delineating our different approaches to Morrison. First, Holloway will begin with a piece of how Morrison's older Black women triggered memories of Black matriarchs of her childhood and how these women stand as sources for her spiritual strength. She will also discuss the Black extended family and these women's place in that tradition. Holloway will establish the way that African archetypes surface in Morrison's women. Secondly, Demetrakopoulos will discuss her feelings of connection to the image of the Black matriarch and how this image in Morrison resonates with goddess imagery from her past, extending that imagery and strengthening it. Demetrakopoulos will discuss how these old women establish and instruct younger women in terms of spiritual wisdom that is specifically female. Thirdly, Holloway will discuss how men need the wisdom of the Black matriarch and how Morrison illustrates the availability of that wisdom. In our conclusion, we will return to our collective ''we'' voice.

A REVERIE ON MORRISON
AND BLACK FEMALE MEMORY—HOLLOWAY

Reading Morrison reminds me of listening to a tape made of my Great Aunt Wilma. On the tape her voice is weak and scratchy with age; there are points where I can barely hear the stories. But, the gaps did not much matter because I had been hearing these stories from all the women in my family since I was young. My great aunt's rendition is the more exciting, possibly because of the charisma of ''story'' itself, possibly because in years of re-telling the stories developed liturgical significance for me, but probably also because she remembered them so well in the unique clarity age brings to the events of our early lives. As I read Morrison's novels, these stories come back to me—their flavor, their scents and their aches. They are the sources and bedrock of a racial memory that bonds Black women together in our special heritage.

In this way Morrison belongs to a feminist tradition, a Black tradition and a humanist tradition—she merges them all in her telling. As readers we participate most strongly through whatever traditions we bring along with us. Morrison's books triggered my reminiscences and flashes of memory as a member of the culture out of which she writes her novels. The novels stir my memories not only through their language and character and vibrancy, but also through the urgency of Morrison's story telling. Her own life patterns weave themselves around and out of narrative, embracing me, as well.

As I view her older women like Circe and Pilate, Eva and Aunt Jimmy, I see a tradition of women who were not cut as much from fictive cloth as from reality. These women's stories are all different, but there is a crucial sameness as well. Circe (*Song of Solomon*) is fully magical, a woman who lives amidst the ruins of an old Southern mansion, alive well past a century of living. She survives on the ferocity of an anger accumulated as a young woman serving the bizarre needs of a vapid white mistress. The anger sustains and nurtures her into the time when her spiritual healing and remembrance of family will assure that Milkman Dead, the son of the child she saved from white murderers years earlier, will learn the legacy of his family and renew his spirit through this knowledge. Eva (*Sula*) is as real as Circe is mystical—a paragon of strength and wit. Instead of "knowledge" in a western sense of "accumulated facts," Eva has mother-wit, a survival-type wisdom that allows her to sustain the tattered remains of a clan moved too often. She is the mistress of a boarding house where the leftovers of families, hers and nameless others, live on the periphery of reality after society has turned them mad, abandoned them, drugged them past memory or relentlessly abused them until they were emptied of life. Morrison sets the story in the U.S. Midwest to underscore how the clan has shifted locales from Africa to the U.S. South and finally to a heartless "heartland" of America. Unlike the mystical Circe, we know Eva's age, her children and her tragedies. Morrison gives us image after image of the strength of her reactive wit fighting for the survival of the clan. In one scene Eva leaps from the third-story window of her boarding house onto the burning figure of her daughter in the yard below in a phoenix-like attempt to quench the fire with her own massive body that consumes her child. Unlike Circe, her majesty and magic are not absorbed into an elusive mythology. Her name, which means "life-giving," is no mythic goddess reference. Throughout this book, Eva's effort is to maintain life, even when maintenance means her assuring the survival of the spirit, rather than the body, as when she kills her drug-addicted son.

For all of Morrison's women, strength lies in their reacting to their conditions in ways that protect their trusts—the clan, their families. They remind me of Mrs. Smith. I did not know her by any other name. She was to me an ancient woman to whom my grandmother occasionally took some greens when she had cooked a pot full. I was always intrigued by the wrap of braids around her head—they were grey braids, streaked with bits of a faded blue tint, and I remember thinking that they were like my braids and why does a woman so old still wear braids? One day she caught me looking up at her head and she admonished me, "Don't go fixin' on my head, child. You listen to what I'm telling you with my mouth an' get out of your mind to stare at people." Mrs. Smith understood, and demanded my understanding, that her words were important for me. My grandmother knew I needed this language as well. There were many times she took me to Mrs. Smith's home, or the houses of other older women she knew and ministered to, and told me to sit quietly while they talked; I now realize that they never sent me out of the room because they wanted me to listen and learn and wonder at women like them. They knew the importance of their conversations and began teaching me their ways through their words. Women like Mrs. Smith and Eva and Circe—as children we could never know enough about them; we hungered for any tidbit of gossip that hinted at their histories. Imagining some past for them was exciting and different from the lives we knew. We never imagined these women placid and still. We met them at the point of achieved, accomplished adulthood, where they had arrived safe and whole. Morrison draws us back to our childhood wonderings of "how did they get to be so?" and fabricates her stories out of these musings. These women are archetypes of feminine mystery partly because they appear in our lives as epiphanies spun out of whole cloth, although we know they were not always so. The miracle of their survival into old age is our reality, our possession of their presence in our formative years. Morrison's fiction fills in their elusive pasts with stories of them as girls and young women who are in danger of not achieving the miracle of age. Through the language and imagery of her story she warns readers like me by revitalizing the memories of my own past. Morrison makes us remember both the wit and the magical strengths that are responsible for the survival of the clan.

Black women have a specific need to keep their instincts and childhood memories more pure, immediate and healing than Euro-American women because we can grow into the women Morrison has fictionalized as Pilate and Circe, Eva and Aunt Jimmy—women who impart feminine spiritual wisdom, whether we are too young to see the significance or old enough only to notice that "we both wear braids.'' This shared wisdom becomes the basis of survival for our children and finally our culture. Women who heal, women like M'dear (*The Bluest Eye*) who are sent for when western methods of doctoring are inadequate, take whatever smacks of survival, be it African or Christian, white or Black, male or female, and create something useful from it. Nel (*Sula*) is a child, young woman, and finally a mature elderly woman in this novel. Morrison shows how she lost touch with her community through her mother's perverse denial of her lineage (she clothespins Nel's nose to make it more aquiline—a familiar incident for many Black women). Nel also loses her link with her childhood friend Sula, whose family sustains the community (Sula is Eva's granddaughter), even under the most repressive social conditions. Sula was Nel's potential for womanhood connected to clan and selfhood which she abandons to imitate the western role of wife and mother, detached from the community that surrounds her. Not until Shadrack, the community's carrier of mad wisdom, passes Nel on the street after Sula's death is she able to reclaim her cultural link to Sula. Her cry, ''we was girls together,'' implies that they could not be whole women apart. Black women merge mystery and madness in ways that deepen and root their lives, their souls. Their legacy is this depth, resonance and darkness.

When I was growing up, everybody went home for the summer. Home meant South, and there we reconnected to the natural communities that northern urban areas were unable to nurture. The older I grew, however, the more home became those inner cities of northern metropolises. Black people had been displaced from the southern communities. Southern communities were better able to support the mythologies and values of Africa; in the North, Black values were in serious danger because the distance from their points of origin had increased and the physical environments of brick and concrete could not contain or stir the lush and fertile remembrances of things past. This endangered wisdom is what Morrison portrays through the images of her older women. She invests them with a mythic status. In *Tar Baby* they are women who live in trees and who inhabit dreams that are full with symbols of fertility and life. These older women taunt a young woman, Jadine, because she is losing her femaleness, sacrificing it to western values. Morrison presents us with their values and their legacies and questions us— where are we, as women, in comparison to them? She shows us Jadine and Nel and Pecola and Sula as girls to emphasize the danger of being lost from our culture and the consequences of this loss as alienation from mature, communal womanhood. Jadine rejects her past, even when the character in this novel who is the symbolic link between the western and non-western worlds takes her to his home in the South to give her the chance to acknowledge her roots. She rejects his offering because her rejection of her own femaleness runs too deep for her to see the relationship between herself and the tree-ladies, or her sexual and fertile dream women, or the community of women who gather on Sundays to make pies in the basements of churches. She is the personification of wisdom endangered because too many young Black women have the opportunity to westernize themselves so thoroughly that their Blackness, and in consequence their femaleness, is erased by the aseptic masks of western "culture." Black women must claim their lineage, embodied in the Black older woman, mythic or real, to know themselves and to assure the survival of the clan.

The extended Black family, represented in some form in all of Morrison's novel, also reaches into my earliest memories. My grandmother went through menopause in her mid-twenties. Her early menopause was significant in the construction of our family. For us, it meant that grandmother extended her nurturing to several other children, related and not related; and it meant our learning that family was no narrowly defined thing. Instead, "family" was extended through our responsibility to nurture and care for those who happened to come under our roofs, often because their own families had been sacrificed in some sociopolitical manueverings of western culture. In *The Bluest Eye*, Mrs. MacTeer took Pecola into her home and tried to give her some sense of a family that was not destroyed, as Pecola's had been, by poverty and racism. The fictive situation here is an image of Black realities. In addition to extension, naming within the Black family—to have an "Uncle Son" or an "Aunt Sis" or a sibling known as "Brother"—suggests something very important to a Black child growing up in this network. Naming gives us a sense that reproduction need not be biological, and that we have ways of drawing attention through names to the importance of the familial networks. Morrison inverts the significance of this control in *Song Of Solomon*. In this novel, the family name "Dead" is given to the patriarch of the clan by a white census taker who carelessly filled in the blank of the census roles for surname with the status of his father. White carelessness with such issues as lineage illustrates the need for Black attention toward sustaining what community has been left us. Part of our sustenance has meant the acknowledgement that biological reproduction was often stymied by the ravages of racism—whether it was the separation of the family during slavery or the horrific statistics of Black infant deaths in contemporary communities. Whoever remains of the community, however we come together, our responsibility to each other is collective. Carrie Allen McCray writes that "Our cultural heritage, our historic roles in this society, and the experience of oppression and strong religious beliefs have combined to develop, generally, within our people a special set of humanistic values." She traces these values to an African heritage that placed "great value on marriage, family unity, kinship bonds, and responsibility to the extended family and the broader society." McCray notes that these values meant for the slave woman that she would care for whatever children were left after families were sold away from each other. Finally, McCray notes that both the history as well as the culture of the Black woman placed her in the social situation of being responsible for the extended family, a role that "did not end with slavery, but continued to be a major one in the economic history of the Black woman."[11]

There is an unmistakable image of the surviving clan throughout Morrison; especially poignant is the somber reminder of legacy in *Sula* as the litany of the collective gravestones of the Peace clan in Nel's visit to the cemetery. Morrison's emphasis on survival is critical, because here we get a sense that a history has preceded and a future is promised. This is an important illustration of Mbiti's reference to worship of the living, the yet to be born and the departed.

The songs and stories of Black women, especially older Black women, ensure and protect our history and our future. Morrison's singing women are a reminder of certain memories that are historical bulwarks in many Black lives. When I think of my early childhood, one of my most forceful memories is of my mother singing. As I remember it now, she sang throughout my infancy and toddlerhood and right up through my teen years. I am touched by a gift she gave me this past Christmas, a book of Black spirituals. Her inscription on the inside cover was "For my children, so that they might remember." I think of this and look at Morrison's portrait of Mrs. MacTeer in *The Bluest Eye*, who sang to her children as well as to herself. I wonder that these images are not closely linked to all women. But, most of the white women I have spoken to about this tell me there was no singing in their households, or that "singing"

meant voice lessons and something very distant from that spontaneous expression of spirit that the Black women I speak with remember. These discussions reinforce my belief that a Black woman's gift
to her children is often subtle, not just likely to be transmitted in
spoken language but also in song or in deed. The images of my past
are enlivened by Morrison; and the sad note is that we are all in danger of losing that past. Mother sensed this in a need to give a book of
songs when those songs really ought to be a part of an intrinsic
memory. Memory, Morrison points out, is damaged when the community is threatened and its women are tempted away from nurturing its collective values and instead feed the Euro-American "survival of the fittest" individualistic mentality. Mother is critically
aware that her role is to insure that the message of my past is sent in
as many forms as necessary to assure its survival. This perspective
is valuable as we look at Morrison and sense that the urgency in her
writing comes partly from her understanding of her weighty role as
one who clarifies, for those of us who are not sure or who are in
danger of loss, that wisdom and femaleness and humanhood are ir-
revocably linked, and present especially in older women whose very
conditions make the politics of their survival a lesson for us all.

MORRISON'S OLD WOMEN AND THE ONTOLOGIZING OF OUR FOREMOTHERS—DEMETRAKOPOULOS

Although I come to Morrison from a different cultural perspective than my co-author, her characters deeply touch and give form to
my ancestors' pride and my sense of female sacrality. I come from a
blue-collar, mixed-white strain, although Scottish values reigned, as
embodied in my tough, tiny, gnarly, red-haired grandmother, who
lived with my family. Although Eva is a Black matriarch, her image
resonates to my memories of my grandmother. And, as I have read
my co-author's responses and memories about Morrison's women
as Black women, I have been further and immeasurably enriched,
both in understanding Morrison better and in understanding my own
imagery of the Black matriarch more deeply than before. For years I
have had a lyrically wise yet sinewy, large, angular old Black woman appear in my dreams. She calls herself Jubilee Moore and is an
image of inner strength for me. There is not space here for me to
speculate on why a white psyche would present this image to sym-

bolize cosmic unity and comfort, but, I do want to point out that my imagery is of an articulate, active woman, hardly William Faulkner's Dilsey.

Morrison's women stir personal imagery and collective female memory; they also have a spiritual strength and aura that are best expressed for me by my studies of Goddess imagery. In my book, *Listening to Our Bodies*,[12] I chose Pilate as Morrison's best genera. embodiment of Goddess strength in a foremother, but I really feel the greatest personal affinity for Eva, the head matriarch of the Peace family in *Sula*. The desperation and ferocity with which she defends her children reminds me of Kathe Kollwitz's women[13] and perhaps of my own grandmother. The power of Morrison's style evokes the Goddess energy of this foremother whose survival has ensured ours. Since Morrison has a Master's degree in English, she would at least have knowledge of this goddess imagery; I can in no way claim that she had it in mind when she created her women. But, since I do believe that there are images common to the female collective unconscious, I can claim that my white ethnic frame, while idiosyncratic, is valid as an approach to her imagery for me. Morrison's imagery of the older woman gives off the same sacred energy and aura that Holloway and I both recognize. Holloway and I each bring our own imagery to focus on that energy. I think the essential power of Morrison's voice is her ability to evoke a universal response. The Goddess frame is a way for me to articulate how Morrison's images have enriched and extended my female spirituality, so often bereft of imagistic "containers" or focus in this Judeo-Christian culture. Morrison's women strengthen me as I live through the vicissitudes of my everyday life.

Sula: The Peace Women as the Ancient Goddesses Demeter, Persephone and Hestia—Demetrakopoulos

Morrison's *Sula* is the story of Sula Peace, one of a family of women (Eva is matriarch and her daughter Hannah is Sula's mother) who are like the ancient goddesses Demeter, Persephone and Hestia. The images of the feminine that the Peace women embody are ancient, natural and universal. The Greek goddesses and perhaps others such as Kali, the destroyer, emerge as powerful twentieth-century feminine archetypes in these women. Eva Peace is the founding matriarch and queen of the line; she establishes their values. When we meet her, she is already in late middle age and the reigning deity in her household of daughter, granddaughter and various adopted, interchangeable and peripheral male figures. Eva has earned her regal authority. In one of the most poignant and harrowing passages in all literature by women, we see in a flashback what Eva has overcome in order to survive and give her children life. She and her three children were deserted in 1895 by a husband, Boyboy, a man who was abusive and childish. His abandoning her is not a special loss to her personally; but Eva and her children face starvation as a consequence of his desertion. To feed her children, Eva sacrifices a leg and regularly thereafter receives disability money to live on. She loses her left leg which reflects the intuitive side of the feminine, the loss of symbol making and the softer gentler values of the feminine. She is strongly, fiercely, rationally and roughly protective of her household until the end of her life. As long as her children and grandchildren are in her care, her house is organized and carefully run, a haven for her women, who do not have to submit their lives to the caprices of husbands or lovers.

Eva develops a healthy antipathy for the co-equal masculine. She understands that to marry would simply empower a man to take her from her home and territory over which she must reign that the young may grow up. Perhaps an ironic parody of the insane wife of Charlotte Bronte's *Jane Eyre*, Eva lives on the top floor of her house—but not as a walled off insane part of the self, for she combines the deeply sane and cautiously protective Hestia and an overseeing Demeter. These are the two goddesses that I see as most operative, most strongly emerging in Eva. Recall that Hestia is in charge of the most crucial life support processes—such as meals and household heating—critical to survival—heat and body fuel being the basic energies of life. Hestia is traditionally uncoupled, her virginity symbolic of the devotion and singleminded purity with which she tends and sustains the home. Hestia's fire is qualitatively different from Apollo's or Prometheus'. Prometheus' is an industrial, weapon-forging fire while Hestia's is a family or communal center to which one returns for succor and self-consolidation. Hers is the fire of life.[14]

Eva returns to her state of celibacy after her husband leaves. Men remain amusing toys to her, but all her life energy is spent establishing a home that reminds us of the guarded sanctity of a convent. Eva's house becomes a fortress for the women of her line. Her immobility is like that of a Hestian Queen; she scarcely ever descends to the lower floors, but sits on a throne-like wagon device to receive her faceless, nameless and interchangeable suitors. They surround and worship her like the castrated priests of Isis, weak and wispy forces of the masculine. Eva retains her female progeny, Nel and Sula, in her fortress, but assigns her one son the role of the moving dynamic hero prince who will sally into the world and conquer it. Her son Plum carries the Hermetic aspect of Eva's deliberately repressed animus,[15] a repression she consciously chooses in her celibacy, in limiting her world to home/fortress. Hermes is the adventurous messenger, the man forever on the road, an emblem of imaginative roving. But, like the other proto-genius Black males in Morrison's novel, Plum is castrated on multiple levels in his sojourn in the white man's world.

As did the town's mad prophet, Shadrack, Plum loses his masculine impetus and his initiative in the white man's army. Shadrack returns to the community insane; Plum comes home a drug addict who sleeps his life away in a bedroom directly beneath Eva's. Eva tells Hannah:

> He wanted to crawl back in my womb and well . . . I ain't got the room no more even if he could do it. There wasn't space for him in my womb. And he was crawlin' back. Being helpless and thinking baby thoughts and dreaming baby dreams and messing up his pants again and smiling all the time. I had room enough in my heart, but not in my womb, got no more. I birthed him once. I couldn't do it again. He was growed, a big, old thing. Godhavemercy, I couldn't birth him twice.[16]

Erich Neumann defines suicide as a regressive urge towards uroboric incest, a desire to merge with the Mother Earth and annihilate the consciousness causing such pain.[17] The perverse and horrible twist is that in returning home the son appears to want his real mother to become the earth, a benign and vegetative Demeter[18] to whom he can return. Eva feels that he wants to implicate her in his waking death. She has fought too hard to give her children a life that is good and fruitful: The year he comes of age, Eva kills her beloved son. The protective ferocity, the tigress instinct, the ruthless love of Demeter transmutes into Kali, the mother destroyer who forces an end of the life cycle. Eva also kills her daughter Hannah when she sees that Hannah will be badly disfigured and in constant pain from a fire.

The last scene of *Sula* features Eva, who outlives all her children although she sacrificed her life for theirs. Nel, a friend of Eva's granddaughter Sula, visits with Eva in this last scene. Sula has already died in this final scene when Nel visits Eva in the old folks' home and finds Eva constantly making the motions of ironing pleats. She is still making Hestian order; but the image of ironing is also probably an allusion to Tillie Olson's story, "I Stand Here Ironing,"[19] in which a poverty stricken mother stands and irons while pondering her lost child. A passion for physical and household order that contains and mutes the tragedies of life is still in Eva, but in a mad form. She had been the principle of household management, an unrecognized logos in itself. Her rationality that managed, administered for others is partially stilled while an under-visionary irrational feminine erupts. She is feminine madness as Marguerite Duras defines it, a voice out of the silence and darkness, neurotic, yet knowing what she wants.[20] This madness set against the "norm" of masculine sanity is actually the truest and deepest kind of feminine sanity.

Eva becomes the sibyl who gives Nel the spiritual and psychological truth of Sula's and Nel's oneness. She is fully individuated, an admirable old woman. She is Hecate, the Medium, the Sibyl, the Truthsayer who still mothers forth daughters but in a psychological and metaphysical sense.[21] She is an unfrocked priestess, the aggrieved Demeter whose whole line is lost to her but who nevertheless is able to give the gift of completion to other women. I am unable to fault Eva for her life decisions of her acts. Morrison thinks that Eva and Hannah have committed wrong or bad acts,[22] I think Eva is a portrait of archetypal feminine strength that goes beyond the author's intentions. Eva built a life and home as best she could when the only act of free will open to her was self-mutilation (she is somehow responsible for the loss of her leg) or letting her babies die. She does not really cause any of her adult children's deaths; she hastens death to save them from misery. Her life has been economically, socially and historically determined in the most narrow way; despite this, her character is one of fierce protectiveness, gracious regality, magnanimity, deep intelligence and great courage. Her sharp tongue is salt with wisdom. Eva becomes the Demeter/Sophia of transcendent wisdom, the Kali who contains birth and death, the last phase of feminine wisdom that never stops mothering, informing younger persons of deepest truths.

Eva mothers Nel into old age. Nel is 55 years old in the last pages of the novel, the year of entry into wisdom according to numerolo-

gists.[23] It is the year that closes middle age according to some gerontologists. Personally, I prefer the numerologists' beautiful image of
55 as the year that begins the rectangle of consolidation, of metaphysical wisdom.

Finally, while Morrison portrays all the life stages of her women,
the final phases of completing the self in old age are crucial to her
patterning. Eva grows more twisted, but more complete. She never
makes a deep or lasting connection with the masculine principle
through a man, and she is a full, individuated, complex old woman.
Completio may take different paths and different patterns; not each
personality in one lifetime can assimilate the same ingredients. Eva
has moved into an unmanned space in society, in the world, and
become a woman, a person of her own making.

The internal union of parts of the feminine seems to be what Morrison insists on for the last stage of woman's personality development. Nel considers the men she knew after her husband, Jude, left
her. "But now she was fifty-five and hard put to remember what all
that had been about."[24] Remembering her feminine soul, Nel's last
stages of individuation begin as an epiphany of Sula, a woman
whose life intertwined with hers from girlhood:

> Suddenly Nel stopped. Her eye twitched and burned a little.
> "Sula?" she whispered, gazing at the tops of trees. "Sula?"
> Leaves stirred; mud shifted; there was the smell of overripe
> green things. A soft ball of fur broke and scattered like dande-
> lion spores in the breeze. "All that time, all that time, I
> thought I was missing Jude." And the loss pressed down on
> her chest and came up into her throat. "We was girls togeth-
> er," she said as though explaining something. "Oh Lord,
> Sula," she cried, "girl, girl, girlgirlgirl." It was a fine cry—
> loud and long—but it had no bottom and it had no top, just cir-
> cles and circles of sorrow.[25]

This image is the trigger, catalyst and foundation for Nel's last
stages of feminine individuation and self-knowledge. Eva is the
mother body from which this truth and the enlightened Nel issue.
Sula turned to Nel during death: "It didn't even hurt"; the newly
dead Sula reflects, "Wait 'til I tell Nel."[26] And so Nel merges with
Sula as she looks to her own final stage of life.

Sula, then, is prophetic in its invitation to women readers to examine consciously and sharply their alliances with women. Because

many modern women will outlive or even forego important male partners and friends in their lives, the meaning of the predominantly female community in which they will find themselves needs consideration. As many social gerontologists have pointed out recently, we can only begin to know the meaning of old age as many people, not just the strongest, live longer.[27] This is especially true for women who, until the last 30 years, usually died much younger than men. The aged Eva brings forth the knowledge to Nel that all parts of the feminine body must be at least psychologically present for old age to be faced from an ego centered in the fullest sense of self. By embracing her memories of Sula, Nel's feminine imagination has assimilated fire and air and roves the inner universe. Nel is finally the survivor of her world; but she contains, through Eva's intervention, the knowledge of her dead sisters, feminine alter egos, through bonds that go beyond death. Eva, Sula and Nel interconnect in the last pages of this novel, embodying a matriarchal consciousness.

I think it is important that no biological relationship symbolizes the psychic significance of female bondedness that Sula's and Nel's relationship does. While I have found a love and belonging through family members, I have found my deepest spiritual connections with women outside of my family, often women from very different backgrounds. These are the women who have made me grow, individuate beyond my own biology and history.

Holloway's and my uncovering of the aged, ethnic, culturally rich archetypes in Morrison's fiction as our heritage is significant to the literary analysis that was the original critical structure and impetus of this article. We have intentionally abandoned the pseudo scientific and detached persona of much analysis and criticism to testify to our depth of feeling and understanding of this subject, even though the abandonment has provoked arguments that criticize such methodology. We believe that our perspectives, presented in this cultural schema, clarify the potential for such biracial/cultural sharing as well as the power of the imagery in Morrison's fiction to reach through the cultural mythology into our own historical realities.

Flight, Freedom and Survival . . . Holloway

The final scene in Morrison's *Song of Solomon* is a capstone to the metaphors and stories of the aged women in this novel and in her earlier novels. In this scene, we are faced with the liberating death of Pilate, an old woman who, like Circe, lived long enough to be sure that her dream of freedom and the legacy of her ancestors would be passed on to her children. As her nephew Milkman receives this gift from her, Pilate is finally relieved of the burden of this task, a burden Morrison symbolizes through the sack Pilate has carried most of her life and that contains her father's bones. The weight of these bones should, by rights, be buried. Through death and burial man is freed from the imprisonment of life and the shadow or spirit go on.[28] Pilate's destiny, too, is assured through the burial of her father. Her destiny was flight, to join the spirits that had loosed their bonds from the earth. She had fulfilled her legacy, gifting her children and her family with the music of their pasts. Her relinquishing of this last burden, her father's bones, is an episode accompanied by song. Milkman finally learns to sing the songs that vocalize his past and in this way assure his own spiritual future. His is the song of his renewed spirit: "'Sugargirl don't leave me here' . . . and . . . he could not stop the worn old words from coming, louder and louder.''[29] Two birds swoop down to the dead Pilate and the reborn Milkman evoking images reminiscent of the old spiritual, "Lord I want two wings."

Milkman, in a final epiphany, literalizes Pilate's flight and his salvation. He surrenders to the spirits of the air, and he rides it. Images of air and flight embody this story of Milkman's struggle for the reclamation of his ancestral power of positive flight throughout this novel. It had been denied him through his own father's denial of his family and community, isolating the "Dead" family between a Black and white culture. His mother had been rendered impotent through her domineering father and Milkman himself had fallen victim to avarice and greed, emphasizing his individual, but not collective responsibilities. Only through Pilate's liberating death, where he finally re-connects himself to her mystical beauty and power, does Milkman remember his birthright. Morrison emphasizes how men and women both are in need of this ancient female wisdom, as embodied in Pilate. Milkman is the collective male and hopelessly entangles his life and endangers his happiness when he is unaware of the importance of female power and wisdom.

Although my reading of these ancient women differs from my co-author's reading, I believe that the potential for this difference is the strength of Morrison. The schema of women's spirituality is nurtured through a familial, racial and cultural network. For Black women, none of these issues is divorced from the political structures of our realities. Our aesthetic, writes Addison Gayle,[30] is by definition a political aesthetic. In the same way that Morrison writes of the existence of the community as a political event, Black women have very little choice but to read Morrison's events as their political realities. The imagery of the elderly Black woman, the presence of the ancestor that protects and teaches, is also a presence that connects us socially and politically with our pasts. For Black women, that is an African past. Wilfred Cartey writes that:

> the villages of Africa are not forgotten, for their pulse beat is so strong that both animate and inanimate things are vital . . . . The spirit world is alive and gives life to the living: the essential ontology of Africa—linking and curving through ancestor and offspring, man and nature, beast and trees, sea and fires . . . nothing is dead, no voice still.[31]

Morrison has connected those ancestral voices, using all the imagery Cartey suggests is African reality and pulling the rest out of my memories. The survival of this feminine voice, through centuries where she should have been stilled by the burdens of tragically gone ancestors, by twisted remnants of the villages or by women and girls who deny their connections to things past, is the best evidence I can give for the political reality of her voice. Jewel Prestage writes of a "legacy of feminine leadership" that was challenged by the experience of oppression when Black women arrived on American soil.[32] The legacy Prestage documents is assured as long as we maintain the voices in literature, in family and within the clan that catalog the ancestral spirits and assure them their eternities.

The major task for Black criticism is to acknowledge the complexity of texts such as Morrison's while placing them within traditions that are both Euro-American as well as Black and African. Henry Louis Gates notes that Wole Soyinka, a Nigerian critic, poet and novelist of international stature, reminds us of the:

> recapitulation of [the] relation between the individual black talent and Western traditions . . . *'A ò lè b'ara ni tan, k'á f'ara wa n'itan ya.* A free translation would read: "Kinship does not insist that, because we are entwined, we thereby rip off each other's thigh. The man who, because of ideological kinship, tries to sever my being from its self-apprehension is not merely culturally but politically hostile."[33]

Morrison's fiction connects our bodies to the legacies of their conceptions. Hers is an act of affirmation that celebrates the vessels of this conception—the older Black woman—as well as politically stabilizes them within the sociocultural history of African American women.

CONCLUSION

In terms of U.S. culture, we feel our interpretation and analysis are important in contrasting the attitudes toward the older woman in Black culture *vis-à-vis* the dominant white culture; we also show how connections between members of these cultures can enrich both the individuals and the culture at large. Toni Morrison's literary originality has already been established by certain critics. Ours is the only body of criticism yet to explore the depths of her old women.[34] In terms of Black feminism, our essay shows how Black women's feelings about being women must differ radically from white women's because Black culture values the feminine and the aged so much more than white culture does. Holloway shows the African ethos that lies behind this. Although social structures and struggles in the U.S. have often obfuscated this valuing, the background of respect and reverence are still much more a part of Black culture than Euro-American. Both of our interpretations and especially Demetrakopoulos' reflect how Morrison's women can be read as feminist icons, as contributions to the growing canon of "Lives of Saints" for women. Morrison's novels can be read as part of the modern feminine gospel. Throughout the essay we have shown how our reading as a whole is biracial and how each critic's approach has enriched and enlarged the other's. Our approach has been the "both/and" approach that Ann Bedford Ulanov, a theologian, describes as matriarchal wisdom. Our approach has not been the patriarchal reasoning of "either/or,"[35] that would select one of our readings as more right than the other. With ease and affection we have encouraged the other in her diverse reading. We believe this is a natural gift of being women, to respect the other's individuation even when it challenges our own.

REFERENCE NOTES

1. Toni Morrison, *The Bluest Eye* (New York: Holt, Rinehart & Winston, 1970).
2. Toni Morrison, *Sula* (New York: New American Library, 1973).
3. Toni Morrison, *Tar Baby* (New York: Knopf, 1981).
4. Toni Morrison, *Song of Solomon* (New York: Knopf, 1977).

5. Barbara Christian, *Black Feminist Criticism* (New York: Pergamon Press, 1985), p. 48.

6. Janice Hale, "The Black Woman and Child Rearing," in *The Black Woman*, ed. LaFrances Rodgers-Rose (Beverly Hills: Sage, 1980), p. 80.

7. Mari Evans, ed., *Black Women Writers* (New York: Anchor Press, 1984), p. 344.

8. *Ibid*, p. 343.

9. Janice Hale, "The Black Woman and Child Rearing," in *Black Woman*, ed. LaFrances Rodgers-Rose, p. 81.

10. John Mbiti, *The Prayers of African Religion* (Maryknoll, New York: Orbis Books, 1975), p. 102.

11. Carrie Allen McCray, "The Black Woman and Family Roles," in *Black Woman*, ed. LaFrances Rodgers-Rose, pp. 70-71. I write further on this role of the Black mother, specifically in terms of how motherhood is historically a theme, either literally or spiritually, for Black women writers in my book *The Character of the Word: The Fiction of Zora Neale Hurston*, (Greenwood Press, forthcoming, 1986).

12. Stephanie Demetrakopoulos, *Listening to Our Bodies* (Boston: Beacon Press, 1984), see ch. 7, "Femininity as Entrapment: The Older Woman in Toni Morrison's *Song of Solomon*."

13. There are two excellent articles on Käthe Kollwitz's visual art, drawings, paintings and sculpture. She commonly enlarges hands and shoulders to emphasize the nurturing, sheltering elements of her women; she arranges them standing together in fortress formation to protect the children. See Estella Lauther and Dominque Rozenberg, "The Transformation of the Mother in Works of Käthe Kollwitz," *Anima* 5 (Spring 1979): 89-98; Elizabeth Curry, "Käthe Kollwitz as Role Model for the Older Woman," *Chrysalis* 7 (1979): 55-70.

14. Hestia is a very complex figure as are all the goddesses; see my essay on "Hestia, Goddess of the Hearth: Notes on an Oppressed Archetype," *Spring, An Annual of Archetypal Psychology and Jungian Thought* (Irving, Texas: Spring Publications, 1979): 55-77.

15. I borrow here from Jungian terminology: the "anima" is the man's images of women plus his expression of "feminine" traits such as tenderness, desire for relationship, or placing feelings ahead of achievement. "Animus" means a woman's image of men and her expression of her own "masculine" traits such as aggression, achievement in the world outside the family, her drive to principled, logical thinking ahead of feeling-based decisions. The term "animus" is being challenged and enlarged by women writing from within the Jungian tradition; see especially the brilliant essay by Estella Lauter, "Visual Images by Women: A Test Case for the Theory of Archetypes" in *Feminist Archetypal Theory*, ed. Estella Lauter and Carol Schreier Rupprecht (Knoxville: University of Tennessee Press, 1985). Part two of Lauter's essay is titled, "The Animus or The Case of the Disappearing Archetype," pp. 62-72.

16. Toni Morrison, *Sula*, p. 71.

17. The uroboros is often imaged as a snake eating its tail, growing as fast as it eats in an eternal round. It is symbolic of (among other things) the basic physiological process of assimilation, digestion and growth. This aspect of a human being is sometimes likened to something we share with the plants which mindlessly exist on the body of the Mother Earth. Thus Erich Neumann sees a suidide that is non-violent, a fetal curling back into the sleep of the infant, of animals, of plants, as a suicidal regression against the heroic ego. He also calls this "uroboric incest." While Neumann is under some attack for his catalogue of female archetypes (which can be see as anima projections and thus valid for the male half of humanity, although not representing women as we experience ourselves), I think his work on male individuation is still valid, and I find Plum's life in his mother's house as a drug addict to be a specifically male quest for non-individuation. Erich Neumann, *The Origins and History of Consciousness* (New York: Bollinger Foundation, Inc., 1954), pp. 277-80.

18. Demeter has many faces, but this is the side of her archetypal configurations that Plum's simplistic need most resonates toward.

19. Tillie Olson, "I Stand Here Ironing," in *Tell Me A Riddle*, (New York: Dell Publishing Co., 1956), pp. 9-22.

20. Susan Husserl-Kapit, "An Interview with Marguerite Duras," *Signs: Journal of Women in Culture and Society* 2 (Winter, 1975): 424.

21. I write at length on this kind of spiritual ministering of woman to woman in "Colette, Clairvoyance, and the Medium as Sibyl: Another Step Towards a Female Metaphysics," *Trivia, a Journal of Ideas* 4 (Spring, 1984): 62-80.

22. "'Intimate Things in Place': A Conversation with Toni Morrison," *Massachusetts Review* 18 (Autumn, 1977): 478.

23. Faith Javane and Dusty Bunker, *Numerology and the Divine Triangle* (Rockport, Massachusetts: Para Research, Inc., 1979).

24. Toni Morrison, *Sula*, p.165. Morrison depicts BoyBoy and Jude as particular types of Black men that make it hard for Black women really to marry for life. Her literary analyses are sociologically validated by Clyde W. Franklin II, "Black Male-Black Female Conflict: Individually Caused and Culturally Nurtured," *Journal of Black Studies* 15 (December 1984): 139-55.

25. Toni Morrison, *Sula*, p. 171.

26. *Ibid*, p. 149.

27. Robert Kasterbaum, "Exist and Existence: Society's Unwritten Script for Old Age and Death," *Aging, Death and the Completion of Being*, ed. David D. Van Tassel (Philadelphia: University of Pennsylvania Press, 1979): 72-74.

28. John Mbiti, *Prayers of African Religion*, p. 91.

29. Toni Morrison, *Song of Solomon*, p. 340.

30. Addison Gayle, Jr. ed., *The Black Aesthetic* (New York: Doubleday, 1971).

31. Wilfred Cartey, "Africa of My Grandmother's Singing: Curving Rhythms," in *Black African Voices*, ed. James E. Miller, et al., (Glenview, Illinois: Scott Foresman, 1970), p. 10.

32. Jewel L. Prestage, "The Political Behavior of American Black Women: An Overview," in *Black Woman*, ed. La Frances Rodgers-Rose, p. 233.

33. Henry Louis Gates, Jr., *Black Literature and Literary Theory* (New York: Methuen, 1984), p. 4.

34. Our manuscript (in-progess), *New Dimensions of Spirituality: A Bi-Racial Reading of the Novels of Toni Morrison*, extends both the premise of the critical approach in this article, and explores further the imagery of all of Morrison's women—girls, young women and elderly, mature adults.

35. Ann and Barry Ulanov, *Religion and the Unconscious* (Philadelphia: Westminster Press, 1975). p. 154.

Aging: Religious Sisters
Facing the Future

Rita L. Margraff, MA, GNSH

ABSTRACT. Entry of young women into religious orders has decreased, and life expectancy of women in religious orders is above that of the general population. Thus many orders are characterized by disproportionately large aged populations. In this paper age structural problems are viewed through five major themes: retirement and value of work; career changes; housing; medical; and economic concerns. Three congregations have been investigated and each is discussed through the five themes. Current problems, attempts being made to resolve the problems, and key issues for the future are identified.

NATURE OF THE PROBLEM

Our earthly time allowance has rapidly shot up from an average of forty years to an average of seventy plus years within the experience of all the old people alive at present. Nothing comparable to it has been known before.[1]

This phenomenon is unique in the experience of history; both present and future generations must face it as a major problem within the next decades. One subculture of the aged population is the group of religious women in the United States. These are women who vow poverty, chastity and obedience as members of religious congregations. The demographic changes taking place and resulting in the aging of our population have affected these women and these congregations. In some sense, the impact has been greater on them than on the general population. The result within, and between, religious congregations is the surfacing of issues which have never before confronted religious women. Throughout the following discussion it will become evident that some of the issues can be viewed as ex-

An earlier version of this paper "Aging in Religious Congregations" was presented to the annual meeting of the Northeast Gerontological Society, Philadelphia, 1984.

35

tremely personal, others demand political decision making and strategizing by the total congregations.

The U.S. population is determined to be aged since more than 7% of its population is over age 65.[2] By these criteria, the typical religious congregation in the contemporary U.S. is certainly aged. The author's congregation, Grey Nuns of the Sacred Heart, is composed of 250 members. Of these, in 1985, 29% are over age 70; 44% are over age 60; 27% are between 50 and 59; only 5% are between 30 and 39 years of age. Another congregation, the Sisters of Saint Francis, had similar statistics as early as 1969. Then, 25% of their members were over 65 and only 15% under 30.[3] Other statistics show that in the U.S. in 1969, 33.3% of sisters were 60 plus, 23.3% between 45 and 59; 26.4% between 30 and 44; and only 17.1% between 17 and 29. In 1955, the percentage of sisters sixty and over was 27.5 and that of sisters under 30, 23.5. In just 14 years, from 1955 to 1969, the group of aged sisters had increased almost 6% while a similar decrease in per cent occurred in the younger group.[4] Con Fecher further points out the importance of noting "that 60% of sisters are over 50 years of age as against 40% of women in general."

These facts have tremendous impact on present and, presumably, near future congregations. In the late 1950s and until about 1965, religious congregations felt a "boon" in applicants. The newest members, novices, entered in greater numbers than before. This encouraged many congregations to build new structures to house the influx. Vatican Council II, called by Pope John XXIII, in the early sixties called religious congregations to a period of adaptation—to the times—and renewal of the original mission. This was an unsettling time for all and one result, although not the intended one, was an "exodus" from religious life. Many members made decisions to follow another way of life. The greatest percentage of women leaving the religious orders was under 50 years of age. At the same time many departed, fewer sought membership. These two conditions tended to emphasize the already existing fact that religious congregations were aging more quickly than the general population.

Religious congregations are now faced with the considerations of how to care for and provide life satisfaction for an increasingly older population. To create a perspective from which to discuss how this can be done, it is worth noting the following about women religious. They have experienced the same history as their lay contemporaries, having lived through the Great Depression and its consequences. Most have lived through days of scrimping to save money to build the motherhouses, hospitals and educational institutions that the congregations of women religious developed to advance their goals.[5] But, there are ways in which older women religious are different from their lay counterparts:

> Religious women are significantly more educated, with most holding at least an earned bachelor's degree. Their counterparts have, for the most part completed less than eight years of formal education. Retired sisters are, overall, healthier, better cared for, and have fewer actual monetary worries.[6]

Thomas Hickey and Richard Kalish[7] have noted that nuns have a life expectancy 3.5 years longer than U.S. women generally.

Thus, the situation has developed in which religious congregations may be seen to be disproportionately aged, attracting fewer younger members, and made up of women likely to live longer than the average. The problems and issues resulting from age structure of religious congregations will be further discussed in terms of five major themes suggested by Hickey and Kalish:[8] (1) retirement and the value of work, (2) career changes, (3) housing, (4) medical and (5) economic concerns.

RETIREMENT AND THE VALUE OF WORK

Mandatory retirement, or a "retirement age," is a phenomenon virtually unknown in religious congregations. Traditionally, many sisters have believed that they should continue to work until death. A sister retired only if illness, etc., prevented her from going to assigned work. With age she might well work harder to avoid showing any sign of illness or weakness which could force her retirement.[9] Only in recent years has the idea of retirement come to the forefront. An increasing number of religious congregations are planning for retirement; and articles are appearing in religious literature directing sisters to contemplate and plan for their retirement.[10]

The well known Protestant work ethic, which views work as a good in itself, has infiltrated even the Catholic sisterhood so that "the present day religious woman of retirement age" has a "built-in mistrust of everything that is effortless."[11] A basic reason for the attachment to work is that deprived of some basic means for feelings of self-worth, i.e., parenthood and material possessions, sisters seek evidence of self-worth through productivity and achievement.[12] Attachment to work is also rooted in the concept of community. All of her religious life, the sister has been part of a community that shared all in common. Each member contributed to the good of the whole and was housed, fed, etc., because of the contributions of all. With retirement and the cessation of work the sister faces the fact of not being a contributing member and therefore becoming a burden on the congregation, depending on it for food, clothing, housing, etc. No pension exists. No personal funds have been set aside for retirement. The sister is indeed, dependent upon other members of her congregation.

Career Changes

On the average more highly educated than contemporaries, religious women have often been in administrative or managerial positions. Catholic religious women have been in the forefront of the administrative positions in colleges and hospitals—much ahead of the success of U.S. laywomen in entering such fields. Consequently, the aging or retired religious does not have much patience with activities seen as merely "busy work." Religious women are likely to be interested in continuing education, or part-time volunteer work with a community agency or in some artistic, creative or sociopolitical endeavor.[13] However, sisters who have traditionally been assigned to their work need guidance on the part of the religious congregation in considering such possibilities.[14] Developing ways of providing such opportunities must become a part of the overall planning or religious sisterhoods.

Housing

Most, if not all, congregations have provided housing for their retired sisters. Generally housing either is a large institutional type of residence specifically designed for retirement, or is the Motherhouse, the general headquarters of the congregation. Although efficient and cost effective, such housing may not meet adequately the psychological needs of the individual sister.[15] Prior to 1965, most sisters of all ages lived in large institutional settings but as the age of personalism, following Vatican II, entered the Catholic Church many sisters moved to smaller home like settings. Such moves have not been typical for most older retired sisters.

Motherhouses tend to be located in suburban or rural areas. Transportation is difficult and reduces the possibility of older sisters getting out to meetings, shopping or recreational activities.[16] This isolation makes it almost impossible for older sisters to make new friends in their later years. Life in the Motherhouse or a similar situation takes the sister out of life's mainstream and tends to make her dependent and inactive. Older sisters seem to prefer to be where there are younger people; but more and more the trend of younger sisters is to avoid living at the Motherhouse or in other institutional settings.

Medical Care

Many religious congregations have dealt well with treatment of illness and rehabilitation, but have ignored the preventative aspect. Older religious women, both because of their generations and their religious life, have not been attuned to the needs of their bodies. "Mortification," a form of self-discipline deliberately chosen for a motive of self-betterment or for a spiritual growth, "by its very nature, predisposed sisters to refrain from medication, medical care, or even complaining about health problems."[17] False notions relating to purity and taught in earlier years prevented sisters from adopting such health measures as self-breast examination.

Economic Considerations

The problem of finances is a major one for most, if not all, congregations. Several congregations known to the author have calculated the amount each wage-earning sister must contribute to the common fund to support herself and the retired members. This figure hovers around $11,000. In a large eastern state actual salaries of sisters teaching in diocesan schools or working for diocesan agencies range between $5,000 and $7,000. Many sisters are already opting for jobs in the public sector where salaries are substantially higher.

Until 1971, because of the vow of poverty sisters were not eligible for Social Security. It was the position of the federal government that since no salary was earned by these individual women, there would be no credits toward retirement benefits under Social Security. An adjustment to the Social Security system in 1971 allowed sisters the option of joining upon payment of 20 quarters into the Social Security system. Many sisters began to receive benefits immediately as their congregations opted for Social Security. The initial outlay was staggering; but the resulting income has been of great benefit.

Some dioceses have begun to look at the economic problems, realized how inadequate salaries have been, and attempted to make some changes. Money has been raised for the support of retired sisters based on past service. However, the problem of financial security remains. Older sisters worry about the congregation having enough money or having to sell property that has been much a part of their history.

Ways of Coping With Aging Congregations

Three facilities housing older and retired sisters were visited. These will be described along with the congregations which maintain them. With the outline of concerns in mind, focus will be on what is done in these congregations to deal with increasingly high proportions of aged sisters; how it is done; and what it is hoped will be accomplished.

SISTERS OF CONGREGATION A

This is a congregation of approximately 260 sisters, involved in educational and social work. The median age of the congregation is 61. About ten years ago the Motherhouse and headquarters building were turned over to an educational institution and a residence for retired sisters constructed in a suburban area. This residence is home for about 63 sisters, ranging in age from 43 to 93. The building is divided into three wings—one for staff, one for retired sisters and one for infirm sisters. The religious staff is supplemented by a 16 person lay staff. The facility is modern, well equipped and very functional. All of the areas are carpeted with the exception of the infirmary. This area includes a nurses' station, an exercise and physical therapy room, doctor's office, and dentistry and podiatry equipment. In each wing are comfortable and homey living rooms and areas for snacks. Resident sisters seem relatively happy and involved in various activities.

The administrator, a young sister, enjoys her work. She is fairly new to her position and hopes to create positive attitudes in the residents regarding their own health and for the potential service they could be to others. Much of her day is spent visiting each sister in the infirmary and lounge areas.

Except for prayer and Mass in the morning, and meals, the day is unscheduled. Ambulatory sisters are free to come and go as they please. Many who drive make trips to shopping areas and plan to take others with them. There is a need for a wheel chair van to transport handicapped sisters for medical and social reasons. At this time, a physician visits infirmary patients once a month and the administrator, or her assistant, arranges and takes sisters to doctors and dentist appointments.

An exercise session has started; although the initial response was poor, the appeal and involvement are growing. The activities coordinator plans some special event each week. A program involving poetry reading and creative writing has been held to meet the intellectual needs of the sisters.

The administrator notes that the sisters have fears about their own futures and the future of the congregation. Economic concern is high. The treasurer of the congregation visits residents and speaks, realistically, to the sisters regarding the financial state of the congregation, and the congregation president visits once a month.

A low income, Housing and Urban Development (HUD) project managed by the congregation is on the same property. At present, however, little intermingling is seen between the two groups. The sisters have been invited to attend some classes at the HUD project, but few have gone. The chapel in the sisters' residence is open to the HUD project residents and special invitations are issued for occasions such as Christmas eve.

Although the proximity of the HUD residence would seem to provide an ideal way for the sisters to continue their lives of ministry by visiting, etc., most are reluctant to do this. Early training in religious life fostered a "separation" between religious and laypersons and such training is difficult to overcome in later life. Only a few sisters, most likely those with outgoing personalities, have seen the HUD residence as a ministry and as a social outlet.

SISTERS OF CONGREGATION B

A congregation of about 330 members at this time, these sisters have been serving educational and medical needs in their vicinity for over 150 years. About 20 retired sisters share a residence maintained by staff members of medical and educational institutions in the city. The infirmary for the sisters has moved from the Motherhouse to another building in the suburbs. Along with the infirmary patients and a few non-patient retired sisters, the building houses administrative staff of the congregation, staff of a school and the infirmary staff. The building is modern but does not have the same types of facilities as the residence for congregation A. Medical and therapeutic areas are smaller. The infirmary does not have a nurses' station, but does have a physiotherapy room and a large multipurpose room.

The head nurse/infirmarian visits each sister daily, and attempts to listen to what the sisters are saying emotionally and psychologically. She notes that these are educated women, but also women taught to "keep things to themselves." The work ethic has taught them that worthwhileness involves doing and making. Retired, they think of themselves as "being on the shelf." The infirmarian works to help the sisters emphasize "being."

Mass is usually late in the morning, allowing most sisters to participate. "OFFICE IN CHOIR," saying lauds together, is held three times a week. Prayer together has always been a regular part of religious life; and it is of note that this seems to become less important for sisters as they age.

This group of sisters seems more involved in outside activities than congregation A. The adjacent school provides an outlet for three sisters who teach remedial classes. Several other sisters are studying art or music with the teachers from the school. The novices, who are newly entering religious life, live in the building and include the older sisters in some of their activities; local schools bring in students who entertain; senior citizens' groups are frequent visitors. Rides and excursions to shopping malls are organized several times a week. Many of the community days or special meetings of congregation B are held at the building so there is an influx of "new faces" and some different activity to be involved in.

SISTERS OF CONGREGATION C

Congregation C is composed of approximately 250 sisters, 70 of whom are retired. Most of the retired sisters reside in a building that also houses all the infirm sisters and an educational institution and its staff, as well as the administration of the congregation. Some of the retired sisters live in area convents, the traditional residences for sisters, with younger members of the congregation. Some are living alone. The retired sisters in area convents appear to be very active and involved in activities such as hospital visiting, work with senior citizen groups, a residence for retarded adults and teaching migrants in the area.

The efforts in congregation C are to help retired sisters remain as active as possible. There is no "retirement community" as such. Financial concerns may force the sisters to sell the property housing the infirm sisters and to close their school. Consequently, there are plans for purchasing a small piece of property and constructing a residence for approximately 30 sisters. The intent is to provide a functional but home like setting for the sisters' later years. In the planning process, congregation C has approached a smaller congregation (about 50 members) with a great deal of property and a serious aging problem. They had hoped to purchase property from the smaller congregation, build their residence there, and help the smaller community with sisters who are ill and in need of nursing care. The other congregation showed little interest in this offer.

SUMMARY

In the past 10 or 15 years, each of the three congregations visited has established some type of pre-retirement program. All three have developed programs that focus on second careers and preparation for sisters to remain active, contributing members of society even in the later years.

The two congregations with a school near the retirement house use it as an asset. School children are encouraged to be involved with the older sisters and a mini "foster-grandmother" program seems to be evolving. The older sister is also provided with the opportunity to do remedial teaching, thus remaining active in the teaching area.

Within the last two years, sisters have established a group of infirmarians and directors of retirement houses. Most of the sisters involved in this work in the area are fairly new to their positions and feel the need for a support group. The group meets monthly to discuss mutual problems and ways of improving services. One topic often on the agenda is sharing facilities and services. One or two of the congregations have a sister hairdresser. The service eventually will be shared by others. All facilities operate their own kitchens. Some thought has been given to hiring a dietitian who will work jointly for several groups.

In each house, the sisters are asked to help with household chores as much as possible, including light dusting, folding laundry and care of the dining area. Service is strictly voluntary. It was noted that sisters coming to the Motherhouse or large residences forget how to work. They expect to be cared for and are not anxious to become involved in household tasks. Unlike laywomen of the same age and ability who still may care for their own homes, older sisters may have been conditioned not to do such tasks. In earlier times there were many novices; their principal duty was work in the Motherhouse complexes. Older sisters are used to this and throughout their lives have seen this as the way to retire. The lack of younger sisters is making a change in present days so that some of the work must be picked up by lay employees, thereby putting an additional financial strain on these congregations.

Generally, the three congregations see their older members as loved persons, persons whose late years are important. There is concern for each sister and efforts to make sure each sister's life is satisfying.

Challenge of the Future

There is no question but that the future of religious life will be different from the past. There are indications that the number of young women seeking entrance to religious congregations will continue to be small, and thus the congregations median age will continue to increase with the percentage of "senior" sisters. There will be fewer working members than before supporting more retired members.

However, sisters presently in mid-life will, and do, view aging differently. The Second Vatican Council (1961-1964) served as catalyst for changes both in structure and inner life of religious congregations. Concepts of subsidiarity and collegiality have been firmly established. Changes in dress and life style have impacted strongly on the 50-65 age group. It is this group that was forced to make the greatest adaptations. Prior to Vatican II, these women had lived traditional religious lives for 15-30 years. They spearheaded the changes, and their lives changed most radically. As a result, they come to the later years with a different mind set than many of those 65+. Much of the emphasis in the past 15 to 20 years has been on the person and on personal fulfillment within the context of a religious life. These women are more aware of their womanhood, more conscious of their individuality and more independent of the congregation than their predecessors. As religious life lost many of its external trappings members were not able to routinely follow a set of directions. Decision making was thrust on the individual in a way it had never been before. All of this portends that older religious in future years will be less dependent.

Retirement and Values of Work in the Future

Much of the literature directed to sisters in mid-life is urging them to plan for retirement. Many congregations, such as the three described, have initiated pre-retirement or mid-life programs for their members. As sisters seek new, and second, careers they will enjoy more job satisfaction than is currently the case. They will learn to plan and to use retirement and leisure time profitably. They will be more involved in part-time and volunteer work. We can expect to find older sisters involved in home visiting, in senior citizens groups, in educational programs viewing such participation as a continuation of their ministry.

Career Changes

In previous years sisters entered only a limited number of professional areas: mainly, education and health care. Once in these areas, change was not frequent. In recent years there has been a shift in careers for sisters and they are now in a much greater variety of professions: social work, probation, prison work, work with differently abled, with drug and alcohol abusers, in law, politics, counseling, medicine, gerontology. For many these are second careers and have involved additional, specialized, education. Sisters will continue to adapt to change in their lives and will find the shift to third and fourth careers a part of aging. These later careers will bridge the gap to retirement.

Future Housing Arrangements

Growing numbers of retired and growing financial needs will force congregations to consolidate facilities. Smaller congregations will not be able to sustain the changed circumstances caused by aging and will merge with larger groups. Experience indicates that this will be a difficult move.

Because in recent years many sisters have moved away from large, institution-like residences, finding housing in apartments or smaller houses, they have had to deal with the finances of and the practicalities of "home care." These sisters will be reluctant to return to larger living structures even in retirement, preferring to stay where they have been working, paying for room and board. Since Vatican II many congregations have made financial decisions which allow sisters working in the secular world, and paid accordingly, to keep a living allowance. The remainder of the salary goes to the congregation. Thus sisters living in apartments have had the financial resources to pay rent, and to purchase their own food and clothing. Having dealt with maintaining a household, sisters will be better able to do this as they become older and so will age more in the way their lay contemporaries do—among the people and places familiar to them. Only when illness or infirmity strikes will they move to the infirmary or isolated residences used for retirement. This will bring about a considerable change in the retirement house as now structured and may allow several congregations in the same area to share infirmary resources. One group may sell its present facility and rent space from another. As seen with congregation C's attempt to purchase property from another congregation this may not come quickly or easily. All congregations have a "charism," a particular characteristic gift. Argument against sharing and consolidating is based on the idea that it would be difficult to maintain both/all "charisms" in such an arrangement. However, practicalities of finance may cause this idea to be looked at more closely.

Medical Care in the Future

With changes in life style, a paradoxical situation arises regarding health and health care. Sisters in mid-life are more aware of their bodies and less apt to hide behind the "purity" which prevented them from using such simple measures as self breast examination. Education along these lines has been part of many mid-life sessions for sisters. However, at the same time that preventive health care becomes more typical. Sisters are entering more and more into the mainstream of life. They will become subject to the health hazards of stress, diet (rich foods), and perhaps even smoking. Life expectancy and health problems experienced may begin to resemble those of women in general.

The Future of Economic Concern

Economics will continue to be a major concern for religious members in the years ahead. In the past, a sister lived life with great certainty that she would be clothed, housed and cared for. Even when she was ill there was no concern about paying bills. She was never unemployed, even though retired. Younger sisters do not have that certainty. The years ahead are a question mark: who will care for me in my old age? Will there be a place to retire to? These are serious questions; and the answers are not yet evident. More and more congregations are looking for ways to add to retirement money. As stated previously, more dioceses are moving to "make payment" in some way on the huge "retirement debt" they have accrued. Social Security, while helping in the past ten years, is a questionable source for the future due to the problems inherent in the Social Security system itself. Tuitions in Catholic schools may be increased, thereby enabling pastors to pay larger salaries to both religious and lay teachers. Tuition tax credit for parents, where such legislation is passed, may help in a small way. It is possible that higher costs of private education will reduce the numbers of students and consequently not increase the income for paying teachers.

CONCLUSIONS

To consider aging in religious congregations is to consider aging in a rapidly changing subculture in our society. The older sister of today has experienced living conditions throughout her adult life similar to those she will experience in a retirement facility in that she is used to communal living. However, she may have unrealistic notions about what to expect in terms of her share of housekeeping chores. She may be concerned about the financial resources and if these resources will probably be sufficient for her lifetime. She will probably not concern herself much with preventive health care or complain of her aches and pains. Treatment for acute conditions and rehabilitation will be provided. Her spirituality, which is certainly integral to the life of the religious, may express itself more and more in solitary prayer, the free time available for prayer being one of the blessings of old age, offsetting the loss of ability to be "doing" in the world.

The younger sister, however, may experience many years of non-communal living, never desire communal living in her old age, and view the possibility of an infirmary or retirement residence much as the layperson now views the nursing home. Her housekeeping skills may be sharper, with no sense that she should not have to do housework. She will probably be concerned with preventive health care, and with how acute care or rehabilitation services will be acquired.

She may have experienced two, three or four careers, never retiring in the sense of not "doing" in the world, although the paid hours may decrease or disappear. During mid-life she may well worry about how she and her cohorts will support the growing number of aged sisters, and who will, in turn, support her and her peers in their old age. Finally, an important question needs to be asked: who is responsible for the older woman religious? She, herself? Her younger sisters? Professional administrators? Woodrow Hunter[19] reports on workshops involving leaders from a number of religious orders. The consensus was that the individual is primarily responsible, but that all sisters share responsibility within a religious community. Administrators are responsible for organizational structures, finances and staff. Many orders have already begun the process which assists the individual sister in planning and taking responsibility for her own old age. However, care must still be provided for the sisters who grew old in a structure which allowed them little individual choice or planning. Ways must be found for fewer sisters, earning more, to support larger numbers of older sisters whose financial resources are minimal. Younger people need to be involved in this caring project. Leadership and training are needed to develop realistic programs and to make decisions about needed actions.

REFERENCE NOTES

1. Ronald Blythe, *The View of Winter* (New York: Harcourt Brace Jovanovich, 1979).

2. John Hendricks and C. Davis Hendricks, *Aging in Mass Society: Myths and Realities* (Cambridge, Massachusetts: Winthrop Publishers, Inc., 1981).

3. Loretta Vetter, O.S.D., "Retirement Planning," *Sisters Today* 47 (1976): 582-89.

4. Con J. Fecher, *Life-Style and Demography of Catholic Religious Sisterhoods and Health of Other Religious Groups* (Ohio: University of Dayton Press, 1975).

5. Mollie S. Brown, R.S.M., "Developmental Model of Ministry: An Alternative to the Traditional Retirement Program," *Sisters Today* 52 (1981): 326-51.

6. *Ibid*, 337.

7. Thomas Hickey and Richard A. Kalish, "The New Old Nuns: The Changing Life Patterns of Catholic Sisters," *Gerontologist* 9 (1968): 170-78.

8. *Ibid*.

9. Thomas Hickey, "Catholic Religious Orders and the Aging Process," *Gerontologist* 13 (1972): 16-17.

10. Among the various discussions of retirement planning in religious orders see Loretta Vetter, "Retirement Planning"; John D. Zuercher, S.J., "Retirement Is Everyone's Problem," *Review for Religious* 34 (1975): 599-607; Maureen Brinker, S.S.N.O., "Preparation for Retirement Programs," *Sisters Today* 45 (1974): 394-401; Woodrow W. Hunter, "Leadership Training for Pre-retirement Programs in Religious Communities," *Gerontolo-*

gist 13 (1972): 17-19; Loretta Sigman, S.S.J., "On-Going Formation," *Sisters Today* 43 (1972): 540-43.

11. Margaret Ferguson, G.S.I.C., "Retirees—The New Contemplatives," *Sisters Today* 43 (1972): 543-46.

12. Thomas Hickey and Richard Kalish, "New Old Nuns."

13. *Ibid.*

14. John Zuercher, "Retirement Is Everyone's Problem."

15. Thomas Hickey and Richard Kalish, "New Old Nuns."

16. *Ibid.*

17. *Ibid.*

18. Con Fecher, "Life-Style and Demography."

19. Woodrow Hunter, "Leadership Training."

Retirement Planning
and the Woman Business Owner

Jean M. Coyle, PhD

ABSTRACT. Research on retirement in general, women's retirement and retirement issues relevant to the self-employed is reviewed. Little attention has been given women and retirement, and even less to the retirement of women business owners. From what is known of the entrepreneur, and of women, issues which need to be investigated are derived: Will retirement be difficult? Non-existent? Will the characteristics needed for successful business management be directed to successful retirement planning? Patterns of planning, or lack of it, need to be identified and community supports developed in order to avert problems.

Virtually no research has been conducted on retirement planning and related considerations by the woman business owner in the United States, although a 1980 U.S. Bureau of the Census report shows 701,957 women-owned businesses in the United States.[1] Of that number, 42% of the owners were 55 years of age and over, with 19% between 45 and 54 years old. Thus, 61% of women business owners in the U.S. are in age categories which would seem to elicit some consideration, planning, and action toward a retirement, if retirement is being considered as a part of a total life plan.[2]

In addition, 1980 Census

statistics reflect the fact that, on the average, [American women] live longer than [American] men and, therefore, are more likely to end up living alone . . . Elderly women average a longer period of retirement than elderly men during which time they must rely on private and public sources of retirement income.[3]

Revision of paper presented to the annual meeting of the Northeastern Gerontological Society, Philadelphia, 1984.

51

Elderly women in the U.S. outnumber elderly U.S. males by three to two; there are 15.2 million females and 10.2 million males, according to the 1980 census.[4]

More knowledge is needed about women's reactions to their occupational situations and their preparation for, and attitudes toward, the retirement stage of life.[5] While there has been a gap in the literature of social gerontology concerning attitudes toward, preparation for, and adjustment in, retirement for women, especially is this gap in knowledge notable with regard to the woman business owner. What does this gap signify in terms of societal interest in this issue? If retirement issues for the woman business owner are not addressed, does this represent a true disinterest in this group of individual workers by society as a whole, or are these women taking care of themselves in terms of retirement planning, and, therefore, not needful of societal interest and support? Considering the lack of information available on women business owners and retirement, the primary approach taken herein will be to delineate some major research questions on this topic for scientific investigation.

Retirement, as used herein, is the process of making a transition from full-time employment for pay to a status of not working full-time, year-round, as well as referring to the period in an individual's life which follows a career/job and during which the person is not working full-time and is receiving economic support based on pension benefits accrued during working years.[6] Extensive preretirement planning would include consideration of second careers, volunteer work, meaningful use of time, finances, legal matters, health, housing, and attitude toward retirement.

If there is retirement planning by the woman business owner, we don't know much about it, and we haven't studied it. This should not be at all a surprising statement for any who have studied either women's issues or retirement, since "women and retirement" remains a neglected topic of scientific research. "More women entered or re-entered the work force during the 1970s than in any other decade in this century."[7] Not only have the number and the proportion of American women involved in paid employment continued to rise since 1970, but their attachment to the paid labor force appears markedly stronger as more women than men work year-round at full-time jobs.[8] Most of these working women will retire, perhaps more than once in their lives if they leave and later re-enter the labor force.[9] Because the experiences of these women during their working years "lay the economic, social, and psychological foundations for later years,"[10] it is important both from theoretical and pragmatic perspectives, to study the work attitudes *and* the feelings about the later years of their lives of these women in the labor force.[11]

In terms of anticipation of their retirement, "business owners often retire unprepared for a totally different existence."[12] From a world of daily pressure and tension, business owners may face a retirement period with little pre-event planning having been implemented, either because they have not considered retiring at all, ever, or because they have denied that option for as long as possible in terms of their thoughts about the future. "Most business owners either avoid the subject totally, or else they assume it will all work out somehow, once it happens."[13] The woman business owner, unlike her female or male counterpart who is employed by others, may not have the organizationally structured retirement incentives to motivate planning for that period of her life.

Women may develop their own business for many of the same reasons which men do—e.g., independence, leadership opportunities, economics, etc. Thus, it seems fair to speculate that women's attachments to their creations would be very strong and that they might *very* reluctantly move away from their entrepreneurial role and toward retirement. If they establish businesses for other less obvious (i.e., unstudied) reasons, they might also, of course, be reluctant to abandon their managerial positions.

In her study of white collar professionals, Block[14] found that women *did* see their work as primary, that work *was* meaningful to them, and that women *are* economic providers and *do* derive self-esteem or identity from work roles. These findings and still other empirical studies of meaningfulness of work and impact of retirement for women contradict the historically accepted stereotypes about women's attitudes toward work and retirement. With the large number of U.S. women not only in the paid labor force for a major portion of their lives but also, in increasing numbers, the owners of their own businesses, the issues confronting these women business owners need to be addressed through empirical investigation. Empirical data about work and retirement attitudes and behavior patterns of women business owners, especially as compared to men business owners, will allow policy-makers and service-providers to make knowledgable judgments in designing and providing retirement planning assistance.

Some research studies, as recent as the late 1960s and early 1970s, concluded that women would find giving up work less difficult than would men. The premise was that women were accustomed to having two professions and would return to the homemaker role when retiring from work outside the home.[15] Another proposal was that women would more easily adjust to retirement than would men because women's experience was one of repeated role discontinuities and repeated adjustment to change in the life situation.[16] However, other research indicates that retirement may present a crisis for business and professional women,[17] that women are less likely than men to be positively oriented toward retirement,[18] and are more likely than men to express apprehension about the effects of retirement.[19] In studies by D. Jacobson and G.F. Streib and C.J. Schneider,[20] female subjects showed a stronger inclination to remain employed than did males, with work-based social ties emerging as the chief correlate of the wish to go on working in both studies. This author also found that work appeared to be both important and satisfying to business and professional women.[21] For these women job involvement was directly related to work satisfaction and inversely related to favorableness of attitude toward retirement.[22]

A recent study (Coyle, 1985) of women business owners in the United States found that the subjects had high levels of job involvement and work satisfaction, as well as fairly favorable attitudes toward retirement. However, there were contradictions among the responses of the women business owners in this initial sample. Almost one-third of the sample preferred ''never'' to retire and one-fifth of the sample indicated their *expected* age at retirement as ''never.'' Over half—57%—said they disliked the idea of retirement. None of these women business owners *felt* she had done a great deal of planning toward retirement, although 51% *had* taken concrete steps toward retirement.[23]

A profile emerges from this early study of potential difficulty for these women when/if they retire from full-time employment in their businesses. Perhaps, because they do own their businesses, they can *choose* never to retire, thus avoiding entirely the retirement issue. Given the high levels of job involvement and work satisfaction among these women and the somewhat lower levels of favorableness of attitude toward retirement, will these women business owners have difficulty in adjusting to a retirement period of life? Will the presumably high energy levels which they have brought to their work environment transfer to a retirement milieu in terms of the women redirecting their work interests and skills to their leisure time?[24]

If paid work is essentially an instrumental role for women, contributing little to a woman's psychological identity or self-image and not serving as a point of social integration in woman's life, then loss of the paid work role via retirement should be incidental to social-psychological adjustment.

Jaslow's (1976) study appears to contradict any notion that work is of little moment in the lives of most women, with Jaslow finding that participation in the paid labor force may be beneficial for women (in comparison to women who have not been involved in the labor force): "The worker role certainly is assuming greater importance for women as more women enter the labor force, and, especially, as more women remain the labor force outside the home for much of their lives."[25]

ISSUES FOR EMPIRICAL INVESTIGATION

To what extent does the woman business owner reflect the growing labor force participation and work involvement of American women, in general? The woman business owner, according to available data, does exhibit the characteristics of the typical entrepreneur—among them, a strong entrepreneurial drive, possession of a wealth of information concerning her business, and persistence in her approach to work-related tasks.[26]

With the type of commitment necessary to operate one's own business successfully, a high degree of job involvement as well as a high level of work satisfaction would be predicted for the woman business owner (as well as for her male counterpart). If the woman business owner does possess deep involvement with, and great satisfaction in, her business-related activities, will she find it an extremely difficult task to relinquish her entrepreneurial role to assume the role of a retiree? Or, will she transfer the effective business management skills to development of an equally effective and satisfying retirement period?

If individual differences are displayed with regard to degree of reluctance in leaving one's business, will an identifiable pattern of retirement planning (or lack thereof) by the woman business owner emerge? Will she be found to view no retirement at all, instead continuing to direct her business? Is she likely to favor a gradual retirement, under her own direction, decreasing her involvement in the business over a period of time? (This approach would permit a gradual adjustment to the retiree role.) Will she choose, instead, to cut all ties with the business or to handpick a successor and maintain some continuing connection with the business through her successor? Does she, or will she, participate in preretirement planning beyond the financial aspect? Which issues will she consider most crucial in planning for retirement? To what extent would advance planning alleviate the possible trauma of retiring from one's own business?

Several questions about work satisfaction and attitude toward retirement were included in evaluation questionnaires distributed to participants in the first few minutes of the President's National Initiative Conferences for Women Business Owners in 1983-1984. Because no immediate or direct relevance for the questions was seen by staff in the Women's Business Ownership Office of the U.S. Small Business Administration (S.B.A.), coordinating body for the conferences, the questions were not included in subsequent conferences during 1984. Unfortunately, a significant opportunity for gathering empirical information on work and retirement attitudes of *thousands* of American businesswomen was lost. The conferences evidenced interest by the Reagan administration in emphasizing the contributions by and concerns of women business owners. However, the emphasis in the questionnaires was on participants' evaluations of conference training sessions rather than on building a strong data base on diverse aspects of the participants' lives (including their attitudes toward and feelings about the last stage of their lives). The conferences, as events, were functional in showing governmental interest in issues affecting women business owners, but data from conference participants cannot give us much valuable information about women business owners in the U.S., especially in terms of work and retirement issues. While organizations for business owners, male or female, may address some of the questions raised herein, at some point in time, presently those empirical data which would best enable us to provide verifiable statements about the woman business owner do not exist.

With the almost total lack of knowledge about the woman business owner, her attitude toward her work and toward retirement, we can only speculate generally about the impact of retirement on the woman business owner. With the increase in the number of American women who are developing and managing their own businesses, investigations of variables such as job involvement, work satisfaction, retirement planning, and adjustment to retirement become increasingly useful in policymaking and program development by

American society. As we clarify patterns of work and retirement attitudes and behavior for women workers, and specifically for women business owners, so will we develop stronger bases for theorization about the emerging labor force phenomenon of the woman business owner.

REFERENCE NOTES

1. U.S. Bureau of the Census, *Women-Owned Businesses* (Washington, D.C.: U.S. Government Printing Office, 1980), p. 7.

2. *Ibid, Selected Characteristics of Women-Owned Businesses* (Washington, D.C.: U.S. Government Printing Office, 1980), pp. 6, 46.

3. U.S. Senate Special Committee on Aging, "America in Transition: An Aging Society" (Washingtom, D.C.: U.S. Government Printing Office, 1985), p. 17.

4. *Ibid*, p. 16.

5. J. M. Coyle, "Women's Attitudes Toward Planning for Retirement," *Convergence* 2 (March 1984): 120.

6. Atchley, R. C. *Social Forces and Aging* (Belmont, California: Wadsworth Publishing Co., 1985).

7. U.S. Department of Labor, Report 575, *Women in the Labor Force: Some New Data Series* (Washington, D.C.: U.S. Government Printing Office, 1979).

8. U.S. Department of Labor, Bulletin 1880, *U.S. Working Women: A Chartbook* (Washington, D.C.: U.S. Government Printing Office, 1975).

9. J. M. Coyle, "Job Involvement, Work Satisfaction, and Attitudes Toward Retirement of Business and Professional Women," unpublished PhD dissertation. Texas Woman's University, 1976, p. 2.

10. U.S. Bureau of the Census, Current Population Reports, Series P-23, No. 111, *Social and Economic Characteristics of Americans During Midlife* (Washington, D.C.: U.S. Government Printing Office, 1981).

11. J.M. Coyle, "Women's Attitudes . . . " 113.

12. K. Danco, *From the Other Side of the Bed: A Woman Looks at Life in the Family Business* (Cleveland: The Center for Family Business, 1981), p. 152.

13. *Ibid*, p. 159.

14. M. Block, "Women and Retirement: A Neglected Population," *Information Exchange* 1 (1981), 1.

15. R. J. Havighurst et al., *Adjustment to Retirement* (Assen, The Netherlands: Koninklijke Van Gorcum and Company, 1969).

16. C. Kline, "The Socialization Process of Women," *Gerontologist* 15 (December 1975): 486-92.

17. R. Atchley, "Selected Social and Psychological Differences Between Men and Women in Later Life," *Journal of Gerontology* 31 (March 1976): 204-11; M. W. Laurence, "Sources of Satisfaction in the Lives of Working Women," *Journal of Gerontology* 16 (April 1961): 163-7.

18. D. Jacobson, "Rejection of the Retiree Role: A Study of Female Industrial Workers in Their 50s," *Human Relations* 27 (May, 1974): 477-92.

19. G. F. Streib and C. J. Schneider, *Retirement in American Society* (Ithaca, New York: Cornell University Press, 1971).

20. Jacobson, *Ibid*; Streib and Schneider, *Ibid*.

21. J. Coyle, "Job Involvement. . . . "

22. *Ibid*.

23. J. M. Coyle, "The Woman Business Owner: Retirement Planning and Considerations," paper presented during annual meeting of American Sociological Association, Washington, D.C., August 1985.

24. *Ibid*, pp. 8-9.

25. P. Jaslow, "Employment, Retirement, and Morale Among Older Women," *Journal of Gerontology* 31 (March 1976): 212-18.

26. President's Interagency Task Force on Women Business Owners, *The Bottom Line: Unequal Enterprise in America* (Washington, D.C.: U.S. Government Printing Office, 1978).

Health Care for Older Women: Curing the Disease

Doris B. Hammond

ABSTRACT. The issue of health care for older women as it relates to their financial resources and health care reimbursement is the focus of this paper. Federal regulations that affect older women and also the role of the medical establishment are examined. Suggestions are given for policy changes on the federal and local levels and for a redirection of the women's health movement. It is suggested that women tend to be seen as burdens to the health care system and face both age and sex discrimination from many health care providers. This is the disease that needs to be cured.

THE PROBLEM

Health care for older people is more specifically a woman's problem in that women are living longer than men. In 1981 the average national life expectancy for women was 77.9 years and for men 70.3 years, a difference of 7-1/2 years. Women who live to 65 years old can expect to live an average of 18 more years, while men, at the same age, can expect to live 14 more years. The U.S. Census Bureau reports that the difference in life expectancy for men and women will continue to increase until 2050, at which time a leveling off will begin to occur. At this point, life expectancy for women will be 81 and for men 71.8 years, a difference of 9.2 years. This assumes that immigration, emigration, birth and mortality rates remain relatively predictable. The proportion of very old women to very old men has increased faster than any other age group.[1] Census Bureau figures indicate the following:

> In 1900—96.3 men per 100 women age 75+
> In 1979—45.0 men per 100 women age 85+
> By 2000—39.4 men per 100 women age 85+
> By 2050—38.8 men per 100 women age 85+

An earlier version of this paper, "Medicare: How and Why It Does Not Work" was presented to the annual meeting of the Gerontological Society of America, New Orleans, Louisiana, 1985.

The consequences of this trend are enormous if the disabilities of women 85 + remain at current levels. Since women live longer than men, they are found to accumulate more chronic and disabling conditions. The financial consequences of female longevity become evident. Older women have fewer financial resources than men; and these few resources have to be spread over a longer period of time. It is interesting to note that women report both more acute and chronic conditions than men, but die at a lesser rate. Why is this? It may be that women feel freer to report their disabilities or recognize symptoms earlier, but it is more likely that there is a very real, greater incidence and prevalence of illness amongst older women.[2]

Older men average longer lengths of stay in hospitals than women,[3] while older women are likely to spend more time in nursing homes (75% of patients are women), or under home care health services. Women are more likely to visit a physician, restrict activity, or take time off for an illness. Evidence is beginning to accumulate, however, to indicate that women take as long as men to report potentially life-threatening situations such as cancer. H. Brehm and R. Coe[4] reported that older men may use physician services less frequently than older women, but they presumably use more expensive services.

Accumulating disabilities may finally overwhelm women if they are alone or if those caring for them can no longer handle the situation. Five percent of all elderly over 65 are in institutions, but of those over 85, 22% are institutionalized. Most of these are women since women outlive spouses while men are usually taken care of by their wives.

Marital status has an important relationship to income and further aggravates the problem of older women. Most older men are married while most older women are widowed or single with less household income. About 40% of the elderly are age 75 or older, and two/thirds of them are women. Of those 75 or older 70% of the men are married and living with a spouse, while only 22% of the women are married.[5]

Medicare's Role in the Problem

Medicare was begun in 1965 for the purpose of funding health care for the old but pays for approximately 40% of the average health costs. The rest must come from private insurance or the older persons themselves. According to the U.S. Census, the total median income for older women in 1983 was $5,599 while it was $9,766 for men. From this there can be little available for out of the pocket medical costs. This median income places one/third of women over age 65 below the official U.S. poverty level. More than half are widowed; two/thirds live alone, and are dependent upon current income or their husband's pensions. If they worked, their own pensions are probably meager. It is difficult to make a comparison with males since their income is greater and most live with a spouse or in families.[6]

Nearly one/half of Black older women, one/quarter Hispanic, and 15% of white older women live below the poverty levels. However, since white women live longer, they are the vast majority of the poor elderly. Often the "always poor" are joined by the "newly poor" as formerly middle and even high income women deplete their resources. This is often due to catastrophic or chronic illnesses that require costly care. Nursing homes, for example, can cost $3,000-$5,000 per month.[7]

The design of Medicare's reimbursement methods has accommodated the pre-Medicare male pattern more than the female pattern of medical care use.[8] Medicare provides for acute care rather than the chronic care needed by many older women. This nation's major health reimbursement does not cover prescription drugs, eyeglasses, hearing aids, dental work, routine physical examinations, and foot care. More importantly, it does not cover long term home care or nursing home care.[9] What this means is that the health care needs of older women are not being met under our present health reimbursement plans.

In effect, this results in women spending their overall resources down to the poverty level in order to qualify for Medicaid, the state-federal "welfare" plan for the poor. This application for Medicaid has to be carefully timed so that it matches a women's last illness before death. Otherwise, should she recover, she will live with no assets, other than any pensions she may collect, for the rest of her life. The greater longevity of women compounds the problem in that often this "spending down" has already occurred in order to receive funds to cover the husband's illness prior to death. In effect, this can mean 15 or more years of poverty unless she is one of the few with a substantial pension. The federal response is the implementation of a prospective payment system based on diagnosis related groups (DRGS), a strategy for limiting Medicare costs by providing efficiency incentives to providers and consumers.[10]

WOMEN'S HEALTH ACTIVISM

Women's health activism has had an interesting history.[11] Agnodice in 300 BC, disguised herself as a man in order to practice medicine after being disbared from practice because, although a skilled physician, she was a woman. The seventeenth-century English midwives were followed by the popular health movement in the 1840s. This movement joined feminists, women practitioners, and working class radicals together in rejecting the perceived general arrogance and incompetence of most doctors. The movement opened the health profession to women and sought to totally redefine health care. The twentieth century efforts of Margaret Sanger that led to the birth control movement are an example of the influence and far reaching effect one woman can have. In the late 1930s the founding of Planned Parenthood resulted from the demand by women for birth control services. Following this were the struggles for natural and family-centered birth, the organization of emotional support groups by women to help deal with problems mutually shared, to the women's health movement itself. This movement, composed of hundreds of groups throughout the nation, works toward changing consciousness, providing health related services, and struggling to change established health institutions.

Why is there a need for health activism, especially regarding the health of older women? The generations of today's older women grew up during a time when they learned to treat physicians with reverence and awe. During this time they witnessed advances in medicine that made doctors seem like "gods" or, if not that, at least miracle workers. The early twentieth century saw a change from women providing health care within their families (in 1910, 50% of babies were delivered by midwives), to the "professionalization" of medicine after the Flexner Report in 1910, which demanded high standards.[12] It seemed that suddenly women were no longer providers (with the exception of nurses), but rather consumers of health care. Medical schools excluded women, Blacks, and the lower class who were unable to afford the extensive and expensive education now required.

As consumers, who learned to revere and/or worship the male physician figure, women have given health care less attention. There are several reasons for this, one of which is that the old saying, "the squeaky door gets the grease" is all too true. By accepting the little that was done for them, older women continue to receive the short shrift. The insensitive treatment frequently received by older women compounds their sense of inadequacy, isolation and physical decline.[13]

Older women, in general, find themselves the victims of neglect and disrespect within the health care system, their complaints belittled and their symptoms attributed to "post menopausal syndrome," old age, hypochondriasis or "senility." A prescription of Valium is often the answer given a woman, whereas an older man gets a complete work up. Minorities receive added discrimination. The access to health care services for older minority women, especially those who are poor and unable to speak English, is especially limited. Rural older women find it difficult to secure transportation to medical facilities. Inner city women experience fear of crime, lack of money for transportation, or the lack of a traveling companion if frail. Lesbian women find that their mates are seldom acknowledged as significant relations and, therefore, are not able to be actively involved as a support for the sick person or to take part in her care.[14]

What is needed for older women to remain in good health is really very similiar to what was needed when they were younger: a feeling of self-worth, confidence in one's abilities, social supports, good nutrition and exercise, and the ability to adjust to the changes brought about by the aging process.[15]

HEALTH PROBLEMS

Insensitive care by physicians combines with the stereotype of older age as a time of disease and illness. Added to this are the high cost of health care, the lack of knowledge of women's illnesses in later life, and the minimal research dollars spent on these conditions. Drugs and surgery seem to be automatic answers to women's health problems when research is needed into how to prevent these diseases. The research dollar is spent in interesting ways. Breast cancer, which affects one in eleven women, receives only 4% of all cancer research money. Research into osteoporosis, a significant problem for older women—unlike the ongoing research into heart disease, cardiovascular disease, hypertension, types of cancer, and diabetes—has not improved much in the past ten years.[16] Alternatives to the disease model of menopause need to be explored and tested[17] in order to achieve optimal health at menopause.[18] The discomforts of menopause, experienced severely enough by 20% of

women to be brought to the attention of physicians, result in a patho-
logical diagnosis requiring hormonal treatment, tranquilizers or surgery.[19] Hysterectomies are still being performed by surgeons as a
solution to menopausal discomfort although studies show that 40%
of these operations are not needed.

Because of the impact on so many older women of breast cancer,
uterine cancer, osteoporosis, hypertension, stroke, diabetes, arthri-
tis, urinary incontinence and Alzheimer's Disease, research must be
conducted on their prevention and treatment. More needs to be
known about hypothermia and heat stroke, the use of estrogens, hysterectomies and mastectomies, along with a better understanding of
menopause. Yet, what has the track record been? Medical textbooks
provide "unisex" coverage, as if there were no differences between
the aging of men and women.[20] Many research studies have excluded women altogether. There are probably many who are unaware that the Baltimore Longitudinal Study of Aging did not include women until 1978, having examined men only for over 20
years. The landmark report on healthy aging, published by the National Institute of Mental Health in 1963, involved only men.[21]

The Growing Cost of Health Care

Overall health care expenditures in the United States amounted to
$1,365 per person in 1982. This is $140 more per person than in
1981. Federal expenditures were $394 per capita, $36 more than in
the previous year, but still only 29% of all health expenditures. For
every health dollar spent, $0.42 was for hospital care, $0.09 for
nursing home care, $0.19 for physicians' services, and the balance
for other personal health care and health spending. Public funds provided just over 40% of the health dollar, 68% of which was federal
payment.[22]

Unfortunately, with all the dollars spent, the health needs of older
women are still not adequately addressed. These dollars provide for
acute rather than chronic care and provide little support for prevention.[23] Recent figures indicate an increase of 9.1% during 1984,
which is actually the lowest inflationary increase in 20 years. According to Health and Human Services (HHS), health care spending
was $355.1 billion in 1983 and $387.4 billion in 1984. The average
per capita expenditure in 1984 was $1,580. Private payments and
insurance covered $926, and government payments were $654 per
capita.

The average length of hospital stays for Medicare recipients decreased from 9.5 days in 1983 to 7.5 days in 1984. Unfortunately, controlling costs has come at a high price—a decline in the quality of health care made available to Medicare enrollees. An American Medical Association survey of physicians indicates this concern, as does testimony before the House Select Committee on Aging and the Senate Special Committee on Aging. Shorter hospital stays for Medicare patients may also mean that these patients are discharged in poorer health. This possibility is substantiated by preliminary results of a study conducted by the General Accounting Office (GAO).[24]

Medicare and Medicaid have become so overbureaucratized that there is a steady decline in physician participation and a continuing problem with doctors charging more than is a "reasonable cost." HHS is sending to Congress a report that contains a fee schedule for 6,000 medical procedures which would result in reducing doctors' fees for Medicare-covered treatment. This would be covered in a payment process similar to that of hospital diagnosis related groups (DRGS). The Federal Trade Commission has in the past, however, forbidden on a number of occasions medical societies from establishing relative value scales which, it believed, might encourage price-fixing. It is not surprising that strong opposition is coming from the American Medical Association.[25]

POLITICAL ACTIVISM AS A SOLUTION

The American Association of Retired Persons (AARP) has become politically active and keeps its large membership informed through a "Health Care Campaign." The November 1985 issue of the AARP News Bulletin informed its readers of the proposal under consideration that would establish the fee-payment formula called a "relative value scale." It must be remembered, however, that most reforms address the male medical model, and although there might be changes, the older woman's needs may not be addressed any better than they are now. The report mentions several options to consider. Among these are:

A relative value scale that would set a formula for paying doctors, taking into account physician specialties, geographic location, malpractice insurance costs and other factors; a "capitation" system, under which Medicare would pay set annual

fees to insurance companies or other groups that provide medical services to Medicare patients; a single fee system, under
which Medicare would determine in advance a single fee for
physician costs associated with a patient's hospital stay, based
on the seriousness of the illness.[26]

Because of the longevity and the particular economic vulnerability of the elderly women, Medicare is an essential component in en-
suring adequate health services for women.[27] The question is, how
can this adequacy be accomplished? Possible solutions should come
through the women's health movement. With more than 1200 wom-
en's health groups throughout the nation, there is the opportunity for
a strong movement dedicated to the health needs of older women.
To date, this voice has not been heard to the degree we hear other
organizations working toward health care improvements, such as
the AARP, state offices on aging and the Gray Panthers.

The AARP, for instance, through its health care campaign has
made its position known. AARP opposes cutting Social Security
cost-of living increases, increasing Medicare premiums, deductibles
and co-payments reducing federal funding of the Medicaid program, and extending the current freeze on Medicare payments to all
physicians. AARP supports reducing the federal deficit by cutting
the fat from programs that caused the deficit: Social Security and
Medicare are *not* the real cause of the deficit. AARP also supports
restraining health care cost increases throughout the entire health
care system to bring them in line with the general rate of inflation,
and restructuring the health care delivery system to eliminate waste
and make it more responsive to consumers.[28]

State offices for the aging have also considered the problems of
Medicare to be grave enough that recommendations are being made
as guides to improving and strengthening Medicare. The New York
State Office for the Aging recognizes that, whereas Medicare was
intended to save the elderly from spending too great a share of their
income to meet basic health needs, the system is ailing and the average older American in 1985 spends a greater percentage of income
on health care than before Medicare was enacted. A document prepared by the New York State Office for the Aging reports that Medicare's trust fund for hospital insurance, financed through payroll
taxes, will go broke in 1988; and the fund's deficit is projected to
reach $300 billion by 1995, driven by a projected 13.2% annual in-
crease in hospital costs. Medicare's ability to protect the elderly and

disabled cannot be restored by shifting costs, either to Medicare participants or to other health care consumers, as some have proposed. Short sighted solutions will only compound the situation. The following major recommendations are summarized in New York State's comprehensive analysis: (1) recognize that Medicare is facing a pending financing crisis and an increasing inability to protect the elderly against rising health care costs; (2) solutions should be tied to comprehensive reform of our entire health care system; (3) the government should have an active role in promoting health care reform that is equitable and not dependent on competitive market forces alone; (4) Medicare reform must be conducted with the full participation of state governments whose health delivery and financing system will be affected; (5) Medicare reform must include measures to ensure adequate protection for the elderly against rising health care costs; (6) efforts to reduce the utilization of health care by the elderly should be approached with caution in order to avoid any detrimental impact on the health status of older persons; and (7) debate regarding Medicare reform must not be carried out in a crisis environment, but should involve an education effort to inform the public of the problems and a national study commission to develop a detailed plan.[29]

Innovative programs, such as the Minneapolis Age and Opportunity Center (MAO), are an attempt at partial solutions to the problem.[30] MAO provides a network of medical and social programs that go well beyond those provided by Medicare. It is funded by a mixture of public grants and private donations. Highly innovative programs such as these may help solve the elderly's health care problems.

Innovation has been a theme for the women's health movement throughout the years. It is time for political activism aimed at reorganizing national priorities. More emphasis needs to be placed by government on policies that impact heavily upon the elderly.

The time is now for the energies of women to be spent addressing the very important concerns of older women's health. Women's political activism to reform Medicare is part of the solution, but there are other things women can do. Younger women must begin to plan for their futures within the health care system. Planned Parenthood, an organization supportive of women's health, needs to supplement its education and training programs to include the needs of aging women, or a new organization must be formed to do so. Working within an existing structure would seem to be preferable because a foundation is already in place. To date, however, not much is happening of this nature in the Planned Parenthood clinics throughout the nation. Since 80% of health care workers are women and nearly 100% of extra-market caretakers (unpaid workers in the home caring for sick family members) are women,[31] it would seem that feminists who are professionals in health care fields should be at the forefront of those whose efforts are to impact upon the sexist models and stereotypes still in place.[32]

Ways must be found to assist older women to improve as needed their self-concepts and, perhaps through assertiveness training and other counseling methods, to claim the ownership of their own bodies which will allow them to question the reverence and awe previously associated with physicians. Improvement of self-concepts, which must include an added knowledge not only of themselves but of the health care system as well, will give older women the courage to question, rather than accept as divine intervention the pronouncements of physicians.

Specific measures that could be taken by women include: the preparation of an action packet; public hearings and press conferences; letter-writing campaigns; mass meetings; and considerable effort toward involving the media in issues that should be considered newsworthy. Joining with Maggie Kuhn and the Gray Panthers[33] in efforts to expose abuses and to insure that the health needs of all older Americans—even if they are "unprofitable" Medicare recipients—are met, and met from a feminist perspective especially if the recipients are women, is essential.

A long term goal, which other industrial democracies have achieved, is the creation of a national health service. Whether the United States moves toward such a service, or develops other methods to meet the health needs of older women, feminists must be involved in these efforts if they are to represent women fairly. The fact remains, and history substantiates, that it is only through women themselves, that the best solution will be found.

REFERENCE NOTES

1. Myrna Lewis, "Older Women and Health: An Overview." *Women & Health,* 10:2-3 (1985) : 1-16.

2. *Ibid.*

3. Helen I. Marieskind, *Women in the Health System: Patients, Providers, and Programs,* (St. Louis: C.V. Mosby Co., 1980).

4. H.P. Brehm & R.M. Coe, *Medical Care for the Aged: From Social Problem to Federal Program*, (New York: Praeger, 1980).

5. Coalition on Women and the Budget, *Inequality of Sacrifice: The Impact of the Reagan Budget on Women*, (Washington, D.C.: National Women's Law Center, 1983).

6. A.S. Kasper & E. Soldinger, "Falling Between the Cracks: How Health Insurance Discriminates Against Women," *Women & Health* 8:4 (1983): 42-52.

7. Myrna Lewis, "Older Women and Health."

8. H. Brehm and R. Coe, *Medical Care for the Aged.*

9. Myrna Lewis, "Older Women and Health."

10. D.M. Brodsky and O.E. Ezell, "The Impact of Recent Medicare Reforms on the Behavior of Health Care Consumers and Providers," paper presented to the annual meeting of the Gerontological Society of America, New Orleans, Louisiana, 1985.

11. Helen Marieskind, *Women in the Health System.*

12. Myrna Lewis, "Older Women and Health."

13. G. Corea, *The Hidden Malpractice: How American Medicine Treats Women as Patients and Professions*, (New York: Harcourt Brace Jovanovich, 1978).

14. Myrna Lewis, "Older Women and Health."

15. Ethel Kahn, "The Women's Movement and Older Women's Health: Issues and Policy Implications," *Women & Health* 9:4 (1984): 87-100.

16. Jane Porcino, *Growing Older, Getting Better: A Handbook for Women in the Second Half of Life*, (Reading, Massachusetts: Addison-Wesley Publishing Co., 1983).

17. Ethel Kahn, "Women's Movement and Older Women's Health."

18. R. Reitz, *Menopause: A Positive Approach* (New York: Penguin, 1979); B. Seaman and G. Seaman, *Women and the Crisis in Sex Hormones*, (New York: Bantam, 1977).

19. Ethel Kahn, "Women's Movement and Older Women's Health."

20. Myrna Lewis, "Older Women and Health."

21. J.E. Birren, et al., "Human Aging: A Biological and Behavioral Study," U.S. Public Health Service Publication No. 986 (Washington, D.C.: U.S. Government Printing Office, 1963. Rpr. 1971, 1974).

22. R.M. Gibson, D.R., Waldo and K. R. Levit, "National Health Expenditures, 1982," *Health Care Financing Review* 5:1 (1982): 1-31.

23. Ethel Kahn, "Women's Movement and Older Women's Health."

24. D. Brodsky and O. Ezell, "Impact of Recent Medicare Reforms."

25. American Association of Retired Persons, "Medicare Physicians May Face Cost Reforms with New 'Value Scale,'" AARP News Bulletin 26:10 (1985): 1,7.

26. *Ibid.*

27. Helen Marieskind, *Women in the Health System.*

28. American Association of Retired Persons, "Health Care Campaign," *Update*, (Washington, D.C., 1985).

29. New York State Office on Aging, "Recommendations From Medicare: Analysis and Recommendations for Reform" (Albany, New York: 1985).

30. Ann Curley and Elliot Carlson, "Now You See It, Now You Don't," *Modern Maturity* (April 1985): 32-36.

31. Helen Marieskind, *Women in the Health System.*

32. Marilyn Bell, "Curing the Disease, Empowering Women in Health," paper presented to the annual meeting of the Gerontological Society of America, New Orleans, Louisiana, 1985.

33. Maggie Kuhn, "Gray Panthers Project Fund," Philadelphia, 1985.

Older Women, Policy and Politics: An Annotated Bibliography

Terri A. Eisler, PhD

Social, economic and health policies directed toward the elderly are related to the economy and reflect the basic structure of society in the U.S. with regard to the distribution of goods and services within it. As inequities exist in our society, they are exacerbated in old age and increase the disparities that exist between different groups of elderly.

Although public benefits to the elderly have increased, they do not appear to be targeted for the "worst off" groups, but rather are designed for an aging population that is healthy and financially well-off. Low income elderly, older women and minority elderly are among these "worst off" groups. Older women in particular constitute a growing population of poor and downwardly mobile. The decline in poverty is not visible for either older women or minorities. Income disparities can be attributed to pension and retirement benefits that directly reflect the discrepancy in life-time earnings between men and women and across social lines. Federal policies tend to benefit a minority of comfortable, healthy elderly, while leaving a majority to either scrape by or live desolate, isolated lives.

The following is an annotated bibliography of current publication on older women and politics. Although limited, the citations reflect specific works comparing older women in the United States, Great Britain, Eastern Europe and Sweden, and discussions of social, economic and political policies on the status of older women. The references dealing with the economic status of middle-aged widows and the repercussions of current fiscal austerity on aging are particularly useful, in that each presents a critical examination of the effects of public policy on the elderly, and the older women in particular.

Books

Estes, Carroll and Newcome, Robert, and Associates. *Fiscal Austerity and Aging*, Beverly Hills, California: Sage Library of Social Research, 1983.

Describes in detail the effects of shifting government policies towards the elderly, the rationale behind these shifts and the serious repercussions the new federalism has on older women, minorities and low-income elderly.

Chapters

Thompson, S. B. "Economic Status of Late Middle-Aged Widows." In *Transitions of Aging*. Edited by N. Datan and N. Lohmann. New York: Academic Press, 1980.

An in depth portrayal of the vulnerability of women widowed in middle age. Labor force participation and income from employment are crucial aspects of a widow's life, but by no means guarantee her economic well being or financial independence.

Arling, S. and McAuley, W. J. "The Family, Public Policy and Long-Term Care." In *Independent Aging*. Edited by William Quinn and George Hughston. Rockville, Maryland: Aspen Publications, 1984.

Discussion of an often omitted issue: public policy, and its effects on the formal and informal support systems for the elderly, are included along with data on family care givers and their participation in the long-term care of the elderly.   ˙

Articles, Papers and Reports

Barrett, Nancy S. "Women as Workers." Paper presented to the National Conference on Women, the Economy, and Public Policy, Washington, D.C., 1984.

This examination of structural changes in the U.S. economy and their effect on the role of working women presents a policy agenda for alleviating some of the economic strains facing today's working women. Material is arranged into three parts. Part one provides an historical backdrop and discusses women's shift out of housework, women as providers, and the social and institutional environment. Part two focuses on problems facing today's working women including inequity in pay; climbing poverty rates among female headed households; a high and growing incidence of poverty among elderly women; a lack of support services, most notably child care and care for the elderly; lack of flexibility in work arrangements to accommodate family responsibilities; low pay rates and absence of fringe benefits for part-time workers; and inequities in tax laws, social security and pension plans.

Part three, policy agenda for working women, presents specific policy recommendations supporting increases in full employment; employment opportunities; pay equity; child care and other support services; alternative work schedules; tax, social security and pension equity; and a restructuring of the welfare system. Tables showing labor force participation rates of women from 1950-1982, probability of labor force entry and exit by females 16 years of age and older, and percentage rates of employed workers on part-time schedules are also included.

Blau, Zena Smith; Oser, George T.; Stephens, Richard C. "Older Workers: Current Status and Future Prospects." *Research in the Sociology of Work* 2, (1983): 101-24.

Retirement from the labor force at age 65 is a social institution rather than a biological necessity; it is encouraged by the availability of Social Security benefits and private pensions, and by earnings ceilings for workers aged 65-72 connected with the Social Security system. A smaller percent of the age 65+ population is employed, and older workers are differently distributed among occupations and more likely to work part-time. Telephone interview data from 2,672 Texas men and women aged 55+ show full-time employment to be a deviant position for workers over 65. Return to the labor force is fairly common, and is typically motivated by noneconomic considerations; however, the Social Security earned-income limitations are a substantial disincentive to work. A number of studies have reported an increase in male employment after age 72, when the limitations cease to pertain. Health does not appear to be an important cause of retirement. Early retirement in particular is explained best by the availability of Social Security benefits and pensions. Public policy changes favoring continued employment after 65 need to be investigated.

Crossman, Donna K. "Social Policies for Aging Women." Paper presented to the Conference of the North Central Sociological Association, 1981.

Social policies for the aged in the United States have failed. Socially constructed and maintained attitudes toward the aging population held by the dominant population generate a structural barrier against the aged and prevent effective integration of the aged minority into the economic, political and social dimensions of society. The negative effect of such pervasive segregation is even greater for aging women in this culture. Forced retirement causes formerly employed women (and men) to become economically dependent on the system. Women who have not participated in the paid labor force (if married) become dependent on their husbands' retirement benefits, on differential benefits if widowed, or on the support of family or friends. Politically, aging transforms its victims from active, valued involvement to a cultural assumption that the prime has been passed and interest has waned. Socially, the cultural assumptions about the aging woman set her apart as a non-desirable minority who is often physically segregated from the mainstream. The role and status of the aged female (or male) are devalued by the Protestant ethic so prevalent in the United States: an individual's actual value derives from his/her ability to earn his/her living. By sustaining the idea of appropriate retirement age (for women, age 62), we assign an important human resource, already stigmatized by a natural biological fact of life, to the mercies of our various governmental social policies/solutions (including Social Security, Medicare, Medicaid, etc). We are wasting an important resource.

Daly, Frederica Y. "To Be Black, Poor, Female and Old." *Freedomways* 16:4 (1976): 222-29.
　　Discusses the problems of economically disadvantaged Black elderly women, focusing on such problem areas as age, racial and sexual employment discrimination; health; housing; nutrition; and public policy. Advocates new governmental programs, investigations of the problems of the elderly, and support of militant groups supporting the aged.

Ecklein, Joan L. and Giele, Janet Zollinger. "Women's Lives and Social Policy in Two Countries: The German Democratic Republic and the United States." Paper presented to the annual meeting of the International Sociological Association, 1978.
　　The German Democratic Republic and the United States are compared regarding economic, demographic and ideological differences accounting for contrasting social policies toward employment, education and family obligations of women. In the GDR, 86% of women are employed and a planned economy and state ownership exist, in contrast to 55% of U.S. women employed and regulation by the

business cycle and private ownership. Between 1960 and 1975, the GDR showed a low birth rate and a shortage of middle-aged males due to war losses and emigration. While the GDR's political philosophy holds that socialism cannot be built without the full participation of women, particular ideologies in the United States vary with respect to women's roles depending on class, region, race, nationality, religion and whether the perspective is that of males, females, employers or the government. Regarding employment, GDR women are guaranteed a job, equal pay for equal work, the right to one "household" day per month, and a shorter work week and longer vacation if they have two or more children. U.S. women have won recent battles for equal pay but are still striving to get maternity leaves, on-the-job training and other benefits. The GDR has more polytechnical education for youth of both sexes, and allows days off with pay or full time off to women to go to the university with pay. The U.S. has developed a purely individual and volunteer system of continuing adult education. The GDR has a full program of children's allowances, marriage allowances, maternity leaves, state supported creches, kindergartens, after-school care, birth control and abortion. In the U.S., the private family (unless it is very poor) is expected to subsidize the care of children until they can go to school, and this care has traditionally occurred by keeping the mother at home. In both the GDR and the U.S., women are concentrated in relatively few occupations. More U.S. women are seeking jobs outside the home for economic reasons such as inflation (not a factor in the GDR) and self-realization (also true of GDR women). There is a drive in the United States for liberalized family support policies such as day care, more flexible hours and continuing education; and recent laws have sanctioned equal pensions, equal pay for equal work and the right to abortion. These goals will probably be implemented more slowly in the U.S. than in the GDR as a result of the political and business climate.

Kahne, Hilda. ''Women and Social Security: Social Policy Adjusts to Social Change.'' *International Journal of Aging and Human Development* 13: 3 (1981): 195-208.

Women aged 65 + now constitute about 60% of the elderly population. They live longer than men and this longevity gap is increasing over time; yet their income in later years is woefully inadequate. Poverty status is greater for elderly women than for elderly men; over 50% of aged women in poverty are widows. The social security program, the cornerstone of retirement income, and the lack of congruence of its provisions with contemporary social roles of women are described. Alternative proposals and their possible impacts on women's economic status are analyzed. Improvements for the transition period—while more basic structural reform is under discussion—are recommended. Reform based on societal consensus could increase equity of treatment and adequacy of benefits for women. It is an essential prelude to consideration of long-range financing needs of Social Security.

Kingson, Eric R. "Reagan, Pickle and Pepper: Coercive Versus Voluntary Approaches to Encouraging Later Retirement." Paper presented to the joint annual meeting of the Scientific Gerontological Society and the Scientific and Educational Canadian Association on Gerontology, Toronto, Ontario, Canada, 1981.

A model for examining the two basic approaches of encouraging later retirement is presented in which the coercive approach relies primarily on negative incentives such as benefit reductions, and the voluntary approach encourages continued employment through positive incentives and increased employment opportunities. The degree to which these approaches maximize four policy objectives is assessed in terms of: (1) providing work incentives for older workers; (2) offering adequate incomes; (3) maintaining equitable treatment; and (4) meeting financial commitments of the Social Security system. Costs and benefits of these approaches to healthy and unhealthy older workers, women and minorities are identified. The paper concludes that in the absence of improvements in employment opportunities for older workers, voluntary approaches provide the only equitable means of encouraging later retirement.

Land, Hilary. "Who Cares for the Family?" *Journal of Social Policy* 7 (July 1978): 257-84.

Although Britain has never had a set of policies explicitly labeled "family" policies, most if not all social policies are implicitly family policies because they are based on certain assumptions about the nature of relationships between the sexes and the generations. By careful examination of the detail of the legislation and administrative rules, together with the way in which services are allocated and used, it is possible to expose these assumptions and show that they are not only consistent between policies but very persistent over time. The assumptions concerning the division of unpaid labor within the family whereby women care for the young, the sick and the old, and for able-bodied men (their husbands) is examined. The examples are selected from a variety of income maintenance systems and services for children, the old and the differently abled. Particular attention is focused on the extent to which it is recognized that women are at the same time workers in the labor market and unpaid domestic workers in the home. The impact on their participation and opportunities in the labor market of the ideology which assigns to women the primary responsibilities for caring for other members of their family is analyzed. The perpetuation of such an ideology favors the interests of men and frequently the interests of the economically powerful, but it is not assumed that these interests always coincide.

McCrea, Joan M. "Swedish Labour Market Policy for Women." *Labour and Society* 2 (October 1977): 377-406.

Examined is Swedish governmental policy to improve the economic and social status of women by special programs to encourage the hiring of women in previously male-dominated jobs. An overview is presented of Swedish economy and egalitarian philosophy. Discussion of the economic system includes: economic policy, taxes, worker and employer organizations, and social policy (e.g., medical care, parenthood benefit, group life insurance, unemployment insurance and housing allowances). Other items of social policy are: labor market policy (e.g., National Labor Market Board, the Employment Service, labor market training, relief work and unemployment insurance); education; and immigration policy. Swedish women are encouraged to work on an equal basis with men as a result of the political economy and demographic composition; they are moving toward equal participation in the work force and equal wages, but only in segregated occupations. Labor force participation rates are discussed in terms of marital status, age, family size, education, region and hours per week. The types of work women are involved in are described in terms of industry and occupational groups. More women than before are employed, but the hours are shorter and the wage smaller than for Swedish men. Special programs for women in Sweden include the Kristianstad Project, labor market training, equality grants, regional development (e.g., location assistance, training grants, employment subsidy, transfer grants and transport subsidies), the steel industry, and Kirunavaara AB at Kiruna. The programs recommended by the equality council are attempts to improve the status of the little educated, middle-aged Swedish woman. Although the programs have been successful for the most part, nonsexist education is still needed as well as the hiring of women into managerial positions and increase in child care facilities.

"No, Poverty Has Not Disappeared." *Social Policy,* 11 (1981): 37-39.
This study by the National Advisory Council on Economic Opportunity shows that, in the past decade, some groups have fared much better economically than others. First, the age distribution of those officially termed poor has shifted. Second, the reduction of overall poverty levels has been accompanied by increased sexual and racial inequality.

Olson, Carol. "Socio-Economic Constraints on the "Young-Elderly" Woman." *Free Inquiry in Creative Sociology 1980* 8 (May 1980): 77-82.
Women aged 50-65 have received little attention from sociological researchers or social policy makers, especially single women. Characteristics of widowed, divorced or separated women in this age group are examined through literature review and five case studies. These women typically suffer emotional deprivation due to the assumption that their needs are the same as those of women over 65. A variety of areas for research and for policy development are identified.

Scott, Hilda. "Women's Place in Socialist Society: The Case of Eastern Europe." *Social Policy* 7: 5 (1977): 32-35.
Reports on the social welfare policies practiced in the socialist countries of Eastern Europe tend to stress quantitative aspects and officially stated goals rather than analyze practice. Some socialist welfare policies which are presented as improving the position of women are intended primarily to advance government socioeconomic aims. Examined are the negative long-term side effects of child care allowances, prolonged maternity benefits paid to mothers who elect to stay at home until the child is 2-3 years old, which have been implemented in Hungary since 1967 and in Czechoslovakia since 1971. It is advocated that these disadvantages be taken into account when similar measures are considered in western countries. Examples are cited of the way social policy in the socialist East, as in the capitalist West, has been used to resolve economic problems at women's expense.

Sheppard, Harold L. et al. "Research and Development Strategy on Employment-Related Problems of Older Workers. Final Report." Washington, D.C.: American Institutes for Research in the Behavioral Sciences, February 1978.

The study reported here examines the employment related problems of older workers and develops a research and development strategy for future federally funded projects. Following an introductory section, the content is in fifteen chapters. The first chapter covers a number of critical policy issues and the second concentrates on job related problems of older workers. Chapter 3 discusses the factors and problems associated with retirement. Health and safety of the older workers is the topic of the fourth chapter, while the fifth covers age and work performance. Part-time work and new types of work-time arrangements are the subjects of chapter 6. Chapters 7-9 focus on the older working women, older minority workers and older workers in rural areas, respectively. The tenth chapter deals with employer practices, internal labor market experiences, midcareer change and the role of intermediary organizations in meeting the employment needs of older workers. Chapter 11 is concerned with training and education, while the subject of chapter 12 is current government programs affecting older workers. The Age Discrimination in Employment Act is discussed in the thirteenth chapter. Foreign programs and policies are reviewed in chapter 14. The last chapter presents specific priorities for research projects and recommends projects for immediate support.

Spice, Byron L. *Social Security and the Changing Roles of Men and Women (A Summary). NEA Research Memo.* Washington, D.C.: National Education Association, May 1979.

This document is a summary of the longer document of the same name which was published by the Social Security Administration in response to the changes in U.S. society that have made the traditional male/female roles of lifelong worker/lifelong homemaker no longer apt.

Stearns, Peter N. "Old Women: Some Historical Observations." *Journal of Family History* 5 (Spring 1980): 44-57.

A survey of various aspects of the female experience of old age in France in the nineteenth and twentieth centuries. Improved longevity rates are contrasted with a relatively unchanging, and unflattering, set of cultural attitudes toward older women, as well as with economic vulnerability (both the attitudes and the economics reflected in public policy toward older women by the twentieth century). Adaptability is suggested by older women's emphasis on dependence and on new networks of affection, both translated in phenomena such as new patterns of residence during the nineteenth century.

The Impact of Reagan Economics on Aging Women: Oregon. Hearing before the Subcommittee on Retirement Income and Employment of the Select Committee on Aging. House of Representatives, Ninety-Seventh Congress, Second Session, Portland, Oregon. Congress of the U.S., Washington, D.C., House Select Committee on Aging.

In this report transcripts of panel discussions dealing with the status of elderly women in Oregon are presented in relation to current political legislation and policy. Following opening statements by Representatives Ron Wyden and Don Bonker, issues of social security and income maintenance are addressed by representatives of the Older Women's League, the Aging Council, the Department of Human Services in Oregon and the Center for Gerontology at the University of Oregon. Two articles, "The Payoff Stage of Life for Older Women" and "Inequality of Sacrifice: The Impact of the Reagan Budget on Women," are presented in full. Excerpts of reports from the Women's Equity Action League which include an analysis of the Reagan administration's 1983 budget, fact sheets on Social Security and women, and pension policies affecting women are included. Transcripts of testimony in a second panel discussion concerning the impact of health care cuts on older women are presented. Discussions of the impact of budget cuts on community services, and the impact of Reagan budget cuts on older women, are provided. Prepared statements from Woodrow Wilson, Executive Director of the Oregon-Washington Farmers Union, and from Beverly Lincoln, Executive Director of the Lower Columbia Community Action Council, Inc., are also presented.

Wetherell, Elizabeth J. "The Contribution of Public Policies to the Feminization of Poverty." *Society for the Study of Social Problems*, 1984.

Economic injustice is increasingly a women's issue. Not only are women of color and immigrants getting poorer, but middle class white women are slipping into poverty. Who are the impoverished women and those dependent on them? What is the cumulative impact of public policies lagging behind changes that have occurred in the family and the workplace? At a time of economic hardship for women, state and federal budget cuts have made the situation even more difficult. Discussed is how specific programs have contributed to the impoverishment of women, e.g., Aid for Families with Dependent Children, recent proposals for workfare and mandatory job searches, Medicaid cuts resulting in decreased and inferior medical care for the poor, and Social Security income for older and differently abled women who are in situations that are harsh and undignified. All are implicated in the feminization of poverty. Current global and community responses are discussed.

Women and Poverty: Staff Report. Washington, D.C.: U.S. Commission on Civil Rights, June 1974.

This report begins with a demographic profile. Among the topics discussed are marital status and household composition, female heads of household, general income analysis, the earnings gap within occupations and industries, participation of women in the labor force and characteristics of women workers over the lifespan. The report then focuses on Public Assistance: Aid to Families with Dependent Children (AFDC). This section includes an overview of AFDC and Work Incentive Program (WIN).

Women in Midlife-Security and Fulfillment (Part I). Compendium of Papers Submitted to the Select Committee on Aging and the Subcommittee on Retirement Income and Employment, House of Representatives, Ninety-Fifth Congress, Second Session. Congress of the U.S., Washington, D.C., House Select Committee on Aging, December 1978.

This collection of 18 papers focuses on problems of women in midlife and how public policy affects this population. Discussed are midlife women's futures, role changes, work and education, displaced homemakers, volunteer work, preparation for retirement, continuing education, work and family, psychological factors, new careers, pensions, the poor, counseling and guidance, mutual help, age discrimination, alternative housing and public office representation. Challenges and prospects for the middle aged are explored. Each paper was written by a recognized scholar in that field and is preceded by a table of contents and an abstract of the paper.

Proceedings of the Symposium on Chicanos and Welfare (Albu-
querque, New Mexico, November 19-20, 1976). National Council
of La Raza, Washington, D.C.
The five papers presented at the symposium were discussed and
reacted to by the participants. In "Values, Ideology and Social Services," a socio-philosophical approach is used to compare Chicano
values to the origins and development of the values behind the Social
Welfare System. "An Oral History of a Mexican Immigrant" presents the story of a 75-year-old Mexican woman who, at an early
age, was faced with the adjustments and difficulties entailed in im-
migrating to the United States. A sociocultural approach is used to
document the values, attitudes and motives of a Mexican immigrant
and her family. In "The Effects of the Welfare System on the
Chicano Elderly," the economic and social conditions of the older
Chicano generation are described in detail. A review is made of the
government programs available to them and the effects the welfare
practices and value system have on the Chicano elderly. The theoretical justification for these programs is also discussed. "The Welfare System's Impact on the Chicana: A Beneficiary's Perspective"
describes the situation that motivated the formation of organizations
that would advocate for the presentation of the rights of the Chicana
when dealing with social service programs, discusses the failure of
some federal programs to meet their objectives, and gives case
studies which illustrate problems encountered by Chicanas when
participating in the various welfare programs. The final paper provides a statistical analysis of Chicanos and other Hispanic groups on
the various public assistance programs. The symposium's plenary
group discussion is summarized.

BOOK REVIEWS

GROWING OLDER, GETTING BETTER: A HANDBOOK FOR
WOMEN IN THE SECOND HALF OF LIFE. Porcino, Jane.
Addison-Wesley. 1983. c. 366p. fwd. by Maggie Kuhn. illus. bib-
liog. index. ISBN 0-201-05593-7. $17.95; pap ISBN 0-201-05592-9.
$8.95.

"We're getting older, and we may as well enjoy it," suggests
Maggie Kuhn in her introduction to this comprehensive handbook.
Gerontologist and founder of the National Action Forum for Midlife
and Older Women, Jane Porcino provides many useful facts, extensive bibliographies and addresses of relevant organizations to aid
women in enjoying their aging. While Porcino does not deny the
challenges of the aging woman, the coverage is generally upbeat. As
a mother of 7 who began her PhD program at age 55, Porcino is
well acquainted with the challenges that face the older woman who
does not accept the stereotype of the "old woman." However, her
empowerment is felt throughout the book.

Porcino's guidebook to thriving in old age, not merely surviving,
covers the full range of issues facing the aging woman. Part I,
Women in Transition, discusses many of the roles available to older
women today including long-lasting marriages, postparenting years
and the grandmother role. Considerable attention is given to the older woman going it alone whether it is due to lifelong singlehood,
divorce, separation or widowhood. Porcino's upbeat presentation is
no more evident than in her treatment of widowhood, "an ending
and a new beginning." New beginnings include remarriage and
motherhood after 40 and re-entry to school. Porcino provides
helpful guidelines and checklists concerning financial independence, age discrimination in the work force and housing options.
She addresses the growing phenomenon of the care giving role as-

sumed by women with aging parents and/or a disabled spouse. The coverage of mental health issues (loneliness, stress, depression and dementia) leaves the reader with positive steps to take. Her guidelines for successful consciousness-raising groups and self-help groups are most useful.

Part II, Our Changing Bodies, is the most complete guide to health issues of older women available. The coverage of menopause alone is worth the purchase of the book. Porcino outlines the signals of menopause, possible complications and the estrogen therapy controversy. The information concerning hysterectomy (type, making the decision, risks) is must reading for anyone facing this decision.

Sexuality in old age is discussed candidly and optimistically. Included are topics usually excluded such as older women/younger men and lesbianism.

Tips on fitness are provided in easy to use, list form. The nutritional information is quite complete.

Porcino explains the causes, symptoms and treatments available for the most frequent medical problems of older women including osteoporosis, cardiovascular disease, stroke, cancer, diabetes and others. This information empowers older women to be in control of their own health and become informed consumers of medical care.

Her coverage of alcoholism and drug abuse will be an eye opener, as will her information on the economics of good health (Medicare, Medicaid, Medi-gap).

Growing Older, Getting Better is a handbook for all women. It is a book to read, to keep handy for quick reference and to give to women you care about. It will be invaluable to older women, to middle-aged women who are on the threshold of the adventure of old age and to young women who want to prepare intelligently for their later years.

Della Ferguson
Utica College

OLDER WOMEN. Markson, Elizabeth W. Lexington, Massachusetts: Lexington Books, 1983. 351 pp. Index. cloth $30.00; paper $9.00.

Edited collections can be exciting or disappointing, and occasionally elicit both reactions from the reader. Elizabeth Markson has edited *Older Women* as part of the Boston University series in gerontology, published by Lexington Books. Markson acknowledges the challenge in her preface: "To edit a book on a single theme is always risky, especially when the theme is as large as older women. One must steer between the Scylla of overspecificity and the Charybdis of overgenerality." The ultimate value of this book lies in how well the editor was able to meet this challenge.

Part I, entitled "Changing Bodies. Changing Selves," incorporates studies of the self-perceptions of women, the changes and attitudes surrounding menopause, the role of the health club for women and how aging can effect sexual patterns in relationships. Of particular interest in this section is Cleo S. Berkun's "Changing Appearance for Women in the Middle Years of Life: Trauma?" Berkun begins her research by looking at just how middle aged women perceive themselves and has findings not in harmony with the vast majority of stereotyped images that pervade our society. Ruth Harriet Jacobs gives a unique perspective on the role of the health club. While the quest for a better-looking body is there, she also finds that the health club's role for many is that of "the old backyard fence."

"Older Women in Labor" comprises Part II, which includes articles dealing with the specifics of blue collar workers in the New England factories, the more general needs of women in retirement and the difference from men's of the retirement experience for women, and a historical look at an "old ladies home." The significant article here is Maximiliane E. Szinovacz's "Beyond the Hearth: Older Women and Retirement." She provides a careful review of the literature on women and retirement. Her analysis of the difference in patterns between the male and female experience within the paid labor force, and the problems that are unique to women as they face retirement, suggests that retirement may not be a haven for older women. Some new interpretations are found here as well as excellent suggestions for further study and research.

The section on family relationships provides an overview of several different issues facing women and provides a range not usually found in readers. A unique view of the diverse people who make up the category "older women" is found in the first three articles of this section. The fourth article provides a traditional overview of the issues that impinge on and affect family relationships. "Shopping-Bag Woman" by Jennifer Hand is the first article in the section on family. Hand looks at the relatively new phenomena of women living on the street. In reviewing the experience of the older women who live in the suburbs, that shangri la of the fifties and sixties, Elizabeth S. Johnson concludes that for those who "liked the way we were in the earlier years, we will probably like the way we are in the later ones." Rita Raito and Donna Anderson take the ever single woman from the category of an asterisk and devote their research to her experience. And, finally, Beth Hess and Joan Waring provide the summary review of women and family relationship issues. The strength of this section comes in the articles, their placement and ordering, from the most aberrant of societies' embarrassments to the more traditional views of family relationships; faculty using this text will be wise assigning the articles in the order printed, encouraging readers to understand the impact of aging and the diversity of the experience.

The final two articles in this section detract from its strength and while they can be viewed within the context of family relationships, fit as well with issues of health. One discusses the problems of dealing with parental health issues and the other the denial of death and mourning in our society. The following section, which focuses on health issues, would be strengthened by the inclusion of this additional material.

"Health Issues" is the title of the final section of the reader, and it is an examination of two specific problems. One article deals with the physical changes after menopause and the second discusses coronary heart disease. While both the articles address issues facing women, the section is very weak.

This review started by stating that edited readers may be both exciting and disappointing. The excitement here, for the most part, lies in the articles contained in the volume. Most are strong articles that add meaningful information on life situations and problems facing an aging population, and identify several areas unique to women. The disappointment lies in what is not contained within the volume. The reader has to assume that, unless otherwise stated, the population talked about in this volume is white, primarily (exceptions noted) middle class and that the aging experience is the same for all individuals. Markson in her comments introducing each section tells us more about the cultural, ethnic and economic diversity of women, and promises more by implication than the various sections of the book deliver. Perhaps it is Markson's concern with overgenerality which is expressed in her introductions. When the articles do address very specific populations, bag ladies or health spa users for example, the focus becomes almost too microscopic.

The questions that need to be asked about aging and older women are not answered within this book. Is there research being done that begins to separate the issues of race, sex, class and ethnic diversity? If it is not being done, why not? If it is being done why is it not finding its way into edited volumes such as this one? It is important that as a culture we truly begin understanding the diversity of our society and stop believing that by labeling something "older women," we can understand any woman's experience.

While the strongest section is the one on family relationships, even it does not deal adequately with the diversity of our older women. I am tired of the implicit assumption that we all look and behave alike. I want to find, not hints of diversity but subtantiated diversity within one volume.

Kathleen M. Schwede
Buffalo, New York

THE CRONE: WOMAN OF AGE, WISDOM, AND POWER. Walker, Barbara G. San Francisco: Harper Row, 1985. 191 pp. Bibliog. $14.95.

In writing *The Crone*, Barbara Walker has tied together the strands of history, religious politics and symbolism and addressed the key issues of the grass roots movement of elder women and the women's spirituality movement. She has traced the meaning of elder women from ancient times to the present through meticulous research and feminist analysis.

The opening chapter "Studying the Crone" sets the tone of the book: the power of suppressed archetypes. Next Walker focuses on the ancient triple goddess imagery in " The Lost Crone." Contemporary religions have incorporated, to some extent, the Maiden and the Mother aspects of the Great Goddess, but according to Walker, were unable to revise the wise, powerful, active Crone to fit a patriarchal world view. Thus the elder woman had to be ignored. In "The Wise Crone." Walker masterfully surveys myths from a wide variety of cultures which show law, morality and the inspiration for cultural advances such as agriculture and poetry as the gifts of the Crone.

As "The Terrible Crone" the third aspect of the ancient Goddess is associated with death and destruction. Naturalistic world views, based on the cycles of growth, maturity and decay can incorporate the concept of the creator also being the destroyer. Dualistic systems, based on concepts of good/evil, life/death and light/dark must eject the elder woman; the life-giver and death-bringer must be dichotomized. As the symbol of the Goddess-destroyer she belongs in the realm of evil, death and darkness. Her role included caring for the dying, still a task mostly carried out by women, and preparing the dead for funeral rites, also the task of actual women until recently. Consequently, the elder woman, the Crone, is a fearsome image. Walker points out that "the Goddess-given curse of death is all too real, verifiable by direct observation every day. We are never completely sure that the promise of heaven will be kept. But we know as sure as we have been born that the promise of death will be kept without exception."

In making the transition from the ancient Goddess to the Witch, Walker analyzes the symbolism of the cauldron. The Crone is wisdom and her cauldron the source of life in a circular, regenerative perspective. Walker gives a fascinating interpretation of the Holy Grail as cauldron. As the wisewoman becomes the witch her cauldron goes "from a sacred symbol of regeneration into a vessel of poisons," and the "word Crone from a compliment to an insult." This transition "established the stereotype of malevolent old womanhood that still haunts elder women today."

The wisewomen had been the healers and the midwives but as men took over the practice of medicine it was necessary to stop the elder women. If they cured, without university educations in medicine, they must be witches. The universities were closed to women. Consequently, a woman who practiced healing arts was obviously a witch and evil. In "The Crone Turns Witch" Walker analyzes this transition, the loss of the status of wisewoman, the witch hunting which prevented elder women from speaking out, the developing panic at physical manifestations of aging in women. The image of aging women as evil witches needs to be replaced with the archetypal Crone, "an empowering image of biological truth, female wisdom, and mother right. . . . "

In "The Doomsday Crone" the reader finds ancient doomsday beliefs from a variety of cultures: the Great Mother creates the world and at some point destroys it. Destruction comes about, in part, because men no longer respect the wisdom of the mothers. Walker analyzes changes in the death and doomsday beliefs resulting from development of patriarchal religious systems. She then addresses the threat of nuclear destruction in the world today, noting that "this dilemma is one of the few social phenomena in which humanity's female half took no part whatever."

The final chapter, "The Future Crone," Walker returns to the need for female imagery. The sex-goddess and virgin mother are both found wanting, limited and unrealistic. The power of female imagery is in the cyclic Virgin, Mother, Crone especially the Crone. In the archetypal elder woman, as representation of death, fact replaces fiction, but she also represents wisdom, teaching, healing. She is never old and useless. Her framework is absolute and moral, aligned with the forces of nature, and the logic of the golden rule (found in India and Egypt long before the time of the Gospels).

In *The Crone*, Barbara Walker has skillfully drawn together the myths from many cultures, western history, and the changing status of elder women. The reader follows the changing image from that of powerful, wise, healer to evil witch to useless, invisible nobody. If we turn to the international issues of the day, Libya, Lebanon, Nicaragua, and others, it is easy to apply Walker's framework of patriarchal power as expressed through aggression and war. One can readily fantasize the Crone rising up, pointing her gnarled finger, and saying, "Enough! Boys, stop it!"

But, Walker is not proposing fantasy answers. Neither does she assume that replacing patriarchal religious systems with matriarchal ones would immediately solve all our problems. She points out that our empirically oriented society is not one in which we expect individuals to believe in the material reality of our images. It is, however, a society which knows that "myth symbols are . . . . our best and perhaps only keys to much-needed self-comprehension, both individual and collective. We can talk to and about dieties as if they were real, using their myths to show ourselves the way to our own motives, impulses, faults, fears and guilts." We know the power of imagery to influence patterns of behavior, self concepts and social structures. We use these same approaches to sell products or political candidates.

On occasion Walker's style becomes a bit convoluted. However, the scope of the research and the excitement of the analysis make up for any lack in style. Women who are interested in aging, religion, myth and symbol, psychology, sociology, history, and political science in its broadest sense will not want to miss this book. This writer, who has an interest in all of the above, has added Barbara Walker's *The Crone* to that small, select list of books she wishes she had written.

Marilyn J. Bell
D'Youville College
Buffalo, New York